M000038913

Coaching in the Workplace

Coach Skills for Peak Performance

Tim Hallbom & Nick LeForce

ISBN-13: 978-0-9883236-0-5

TABLE OF CONTENTS

Foreword

At my first introduction to coaching in 1993, I was struck by how beautifully it dovetails with NLP. NLP and coaching hold several presuppositions in common. Both assume that people can choose their experience. Nowhere is this a more powerful perspective than in the modern workplace.

NLP likens people to map-makers. Our internal world is a map of the world. We fill our map with limits and opportunities, many of which are self-created. We can questions the map's limits, or attend to an opportunity, and change our experience of work and life. NLP approaches the complexities of life as a programmer would. It teaches how to craft our choices in a precise and methodical way. As we do this, we create a workplace and a world.

Both NLP and coaching assume that we have the resources we need. We aren't broken; we don't need to be fixed. We can choose our thoughts and shape our internal environment. We can choose actions that lead to desired futures. NLP is interested in how we do that, specifically.

Coaching is a structure to help us make a practice of choosing thoughts consciously once we have learned to. Coaching has a regular, ongoing, consistent rhythm. It invites us to check in with ourselves and attend to the map of thoughts we live in. In a coaching session, we inquire, refine, reformulate and create. We define the next version, or question blocks, or find a way around them, or clarify our criteria for a decision. All these pursuits are greatly enhanced with the technology that NLP has to offer.

I am delighted to see the marriage of coaching and NLP so eloquently described in this volume. Thank you Tim and Nick.

Jan Elfline

Acknowledgements

The authors would like to acknowledge the following people who have made this work possible by their contributions to the field of NLP and to the practice of coaching.

Richard Bandler and John Grinder for their brilliant developments in creating the field of NLP and their models, Virginia Satir, Milton Erickson and Fritz Perls; Robert Dilts, our colleague and teacher who has made so many of the ongoing developments in the fields of NLP and Coaching;

Steve and Connirae Andreas for their contributions in making NLP more robust and accessible; Rodger Bailey and Leslie Cameron Bandler for their work with Meta Programs and criteria; Jan Elfline for her pioneering efforts in bringing NLP into the world of coaching; and Thomas Leonard and Tim Gallwey for helping to create the field of coaching in the first place.

Also, Kris Hallbom, for her contribution of the Universal Cycles of Change and all her great support over the years.

A special thanks to Terry Fieland for his editing skill, and making sure all the T's were crossed and the I's were dotted, Mandisa Fabris for her design idea and Marcia Fieland for putting it all together.

Other books, CDs and DVDs by Tim Hallbom & Nick LeForce

TIM HALLBOM

THE WEALTHYMIND™ 4 DVD SET:

The WealthyMind™ has been taught to live audiences in over 20 countries around the world, and has helped thousands to create more of what they want in their lives. For years now, people have been requesting that this exciting program be made available on DVD, and now it is! This fast moving DVD program is packed with a variety of practical and easy to use techniques and processes that you can use with anyone, including yourself.

INTRODUCTION TO DYNAMIC SPIN RELEASE™ DVD:

How to deal with unconscious conflicts, with Tim and Kris Hallbom

During this special DVD program, you will learn a powerful new way to create deep change in yourself and others in a matter of minutes. This intuitive methodology works quickly, is easy to use and learn, and works amazingly well with children.

THINK LIKE A GENIUS – THE CORE STRATEGIES DVD

With Tim Hallbom

The Core Strategies of Genius are seven proven techniques that will help you Think like a Genius. These techniques were all modeled from people who were highly effective at achieving specific outcomes, and will turbocharge your own effectiveness anywhere.

THINK LIKE A GENIUS – A+ STUDENT DVD

With Tim Hallbom and three straight A students

Whether you are a top student, a struggling student, a stressed out student or one who simply wants to make school more fun, learning these simple strategies from top students will help you achieve more in less time.

BOOKS BY NICK LEFORCE

I OWE YOU, YOU OWE ME:

Breaking the shackles of emotional debt and creating abundant relationships, (2006) by Nick LeForce

COACHING IN THE WORKPLACE

A pocket guide to strategies and tools for powerful change, (2008) by Nick LeForce

CO-CREATION: HOW TO COLLABORATE FOR RESULTS

How to collaborate for results, (2009) by Nick LeForce

HEAVEN IN OUR HEARTS

A newly released book of poetry by Nick LeForce

Overview

WHY COACHING?

People are the primary resource in most organizations. How well (or poorly) an organization performs is a function of how well the individuals within the organization perform. The competitive edge comes from maximizing the performance of employees while maintaining high levels of morale and retention. This requires that managers and owners go beyond the standard rewards, recognition, or typical methods of motivating employees. They need to tap into the inner strength and wisdom of their employees on an individual basis. When it comes to bringing out the best in employees, coaching is becoming the tool of choice.

This book will give you the coaching tools to take your employees—and therefore your organization—to the next level. It will provide you with an understanding of the coaching relationship and how to use coaching skills as a manager and leader. It will help you and your employees to set better goals, make better decisions, take action to accomplish goals, and utilize natural strengths.

When properly used in your organization, coaching can:

- Create stronger manager-employee relationships
- Empower employees
- Identify employee strengths
- Identify employee values

- Set challenging and realistic goals
- Improve employee decision-making skills
- Improve employee problem-solving skills
- Heighten employee commitment to tasks and assignments
- Provide effective accountability
- Tap into employee motivation
- Release employee creativity
- Increase employee morale
- Provide direction for employee development
- Improve company systems

WHAT IS COACHING?

Coaching, as defined by the International Coach Federation (ICF), is "an ongoing partnership that helps clients produce fulfilling results in their personal and professional lives." Through the process of coaching, clients deepen their learning, improve their performance, and enhance their quality of life.

Coaching is an interactive process that helps individuals and organizations to develop more rapidly and produce more satisfying results. As a result of coaching, clients set better goals, take more action, make better decisions, and more fully use their natural strengths.

Coaches are trained to listen and observe, to customize their approach to the individual client's needs, and to elicit solutions and strategies from the client. They believe that the coach's job is to provide support to enhance the skills, resources, and creativity that the client already has. While the coach provides an objective perspective, the client is responsible for taking the steps to produce the results he or she desires.

The ICF goes on to describe the coaching sessions as follows: "In each meeting, the client chooses the focus of conversation while the coach listens and contributes observations and questions. This interaction creates clarity and moves the client into action. Coaching accelerates the client's progress by providing greater focus and awareness of choice. Coaching concentrates on where clients are today and what they are willing to do to get where they want to be tomorrow."

How does coaching differ from other professions? As Jan Elfline, a Master Certified Coach, says, "Like counseling, it is client-centered and individual. Like consulting, it is outcome-oriented, dealing in vision and actions". The major difference between masterful training, therapy, consulting, mentoring, and masterful coaching can be described quite simply. The coach does not have the answers. The coach does not provide expertise. A coach operates from the presupposition that clients have all the resources they need, including the ability to discover and utilize resources.

Coaching allows clients to work and think more consciously and deliberately. It increases awareness of the choices that the client makes and how those choices contribute to the quality of his or her life. The coach provides support for the client to develop capabilities, widen behavioral flexibility, try the unfamiliar, and venture into new territory. Through taking action, clients become aware, at a deep level, of their ability to make choices, take action, and to create their lives. The credit goes to the client, not the coach.

The late Thomas Leonard, one of the pioneers in the field of coaching, suggested that the purpose of coaching is to set more effective achievable goals, accomplish more than you would have without coaching, and to stay focused to achieve better results more quickly.

NEURO–LINGUISTIC PROGRAMMING

Many of the techniques and processes described in this book are derived from NLP (Neuro-Linguistic Programming). NLP started as a solution-oriented model of effectiveness, and was originally used mainly as a cognitive-behavioral psychology. In this sense, it has always been closely affiliated with coaching. Since NLP studies the structure of experience, it can be applied in any human activity, and has been used successfully in counseling, psychology, education, business, law, and many other fields. The initial developers in the field of NLP were John Grinder and Richard Bandler at the University of California at Santa Cruz in the mid-1970s. Since then, many people have contributed to the field. For more information, the book *NLP: The New Technology of Behavior* is a good place to begin.

NLP and coaching are a perfect marriage, because NLP offers a powerful framework for understanding people, and a set of specific techniques useful in coaching. NLP is a field of study, and can be applied in many ways, while coaching is a vehicle to help a person move from the present to a desired future. NLP provides specific "how-to" skills to create change in one's self, and assist others in becoming more resourceful and effective. The table below summarizes the relationship between NLP and coaching.

NLP IS:	COACHING IS:
A methodology for modeling human excellence	A vehicle, and an application of NLP and other communication models.
A field of study	A method of getting from one place to another
A behavioral technology	A skill-set
A set of techniques	

THE COACH–CLIENT RELATIONSHIP

Throughout the book, we will refer to the person being coached as "the client". Coaches are often hired from outside a company to provide coaching to employees. A company's HR department or employee assistance program (EAP) may provide coaching services to employees. However, in some instances the client may also be a subordinate, a co-worker, or a colleague. We use the term "client" to help distinguish the coach-client relationship from other work relationships, such as the manager-employee relationship. As a manager, the employee reports to you and works for you. As a coach, you "work" for the client. It is your job to help bring out the best in the client.

It is critical to define the coaching relationship so that the employee understands the roles and how to use coaching. The main difference between coaching and other approaches is that the coach does not provide the answers. The entire goal of coaching is to bring out what is within the client, tapping into the client's own inner wisdom, strength, and talent, and working to bring out the best in the person. The specifics of the coaching relationship are defined through the coach contract.

WHO PROVIDES COACHING?

Although the material in this book may be used for any coaching relationship, it is intended primarily for coaching employees in a company. The person who provides the coaching and the relationship with the employee will affect the coaching relationship. The coach may be any of the following people:

A manager to whom the employee directly reports:

In this case, the manager and employee have an employer-employee relationship that limits the coaching relationship. The manager-coach will never be a pure coach, although coaching principles and practices can be incorporated into the relationship.

Coaching will be directed toward performance enhancement and employee development. The client, however, will always be aware that she is talking with the boss, and this will limit possible topics and client openness.

Another employee in the organization to whom the employee does not report, usually someone in HR or employee assistance:

The HR or EA coach can function more like an independent coach, but still faces limits because the coach represents the employer. Coaching will still be directed primarily toward performance enhancement and employee development. But this also may open up more personal topics, and allows more openness to discuss the employee's dreams and work concerns. The client, however, will still be aware that he is talking with someone in the organization and this will affect openness.

An outside coach paid by the company to coach the employee:

Having an outside coach is closer to the ideal coaching relationship. However, a coach paid by the organization ultimately has two clients: the one being coached and the one who hired the coach. This will affect the coaching relationship with the client to a certain degree, especially if the client knows or feels that the coach is reporting to someone in the organization.

An outside coach paid by the employee:

This is the purest relationship, because the employee hires and has the power to fire the coach. The coach clearly works for the client.

Of course, the coaching relationship in all these cases depends on the alliance created between the coach and client, and on the coach's ability to build trust. A manager-coach who builds trust and designs a powerful alliance with a client may have a better coaching relationship than an outside coach.

Trust in the relationship with the client is essential to all effective coaching. The coach encourages the client to share dreams, personal strengths, and life challenges in the coaching process. Trust is built by clarifying roles and expectations for the coaching process and by getting feedback about what is or isn't working for the client. A coach who is also a manager to an employee faces additional challenges in building trust with clients. Even with the best relationship between employee and manager, the dual role of coach-manager will impact the coaching process.

The client will always be aware that the coach is also the boss and this will likely lead the employee to censor what is shared in the coaching process. The manager-coach should be aware of and sensitive to this fact. As a coach, it is best to deal with this up front, by discussing how you will manage the dual roles, and the kinds of topics that you can ethically and reasonably address. Usually, manager-coaches focus the coaching process on work-related topics including performance enhancement, managing workplace relationships, career goals, and related topics. The ethics of coaching require the coach to keep session content confidential as far as allowed by law. However, dual relationships, such as manager-coach, may affect the coach's ability to keep confidences, since the other role may require reporting.

Despite these obstacles, there are significant benefits to actively building trust with your employee-clients.

Trust serves to:

- Establish a strong coach-client alliance
- Ease client concerns about sharing issues, goals, and dreams
- Create a foundation for effective coaching

Many elements contribute to building trust. Here are a few:

- Clarifying roles
- Creating the coaching alliance
- Meeting the client's criteria for a coach
- Building rapport
- Professionalism
- Competency
- Confidentiality
- Ongoing responsiveness
- Holding the client's agenda
- Follow-up on previous session items
- Feedback, monitoring, and adjusting the coaching process and relationship

COACHING OPPORTUNITIES

The manager-coach faces two distinct challenges that an outside coach (someone who functions solely in the coaching role with employees) would not have to address.

1. Incorporating coaching into the relationship with the employee. This may include:

   Integrating coaching concepts and skills into the managing role. A manager does not need to define a separate relationship with employees as a coach and may merely incorporate coaching practices and principles into the process of managing.

   Setting up a distinct role as a coach with an employee. A manager may set up coaching times with employees and function explicitly as a coach during these times. This requires that the manager effectively "switch hats" to maintain the effectiveness of each role.

2. Knowing when to coach employees. The manager must identify coaching opportunities to use coaching skills appropriately or know when to "switch hats" and step into a coaching relationship with an employee. Coaching opportunities include talking about:

- Employee development, career development, goal setting, etc.
- Mentoring, employee training, skill development, etc.
- Employee motivation
- Decision-making
- Creative problem-solving
- Conflict resolution

Coaching Process

COACHING TOOLS

Coaching is a complex process. A coach must understand the steps of the process in order to guide the client effectively and accomplish the necessary steps in the coaching process. The "coach relationship mind map" (p. 13) and the "coach session overview" give the coach the tools to negotiate the process from start to end.

The coach relationship mind map provides an overview of the entire coaching process, from initiating coaching to closure of the coaching relationship with a client. It serves the coach by providing a map to negotiate the entire coaching process. The coach uses the map to accomplish the major steps of coaching and to keep track of what to do next in the process. The coach can keep the larger picture in mind while attending to the specific needs of the client at each step along the way.

Most of the actual time with clients would be spent in the circle labeled "coaching sessions." An overview of this process can be found at the beginning of Section 4, on Managing Client Sessions.

THE COACH CONTRACT

The relationship between the coach and the client is consciously crafted through a defined relationship agreement or coaching contract. (In the field of coaching, this is often referred to as a "Designed Alliance," as it is a formal definition of the contracted relationship through time.) This contract defines the roles of the parties and how the coach will serve the client. Coaching is designed to serve the client and the client's goals and needs as they fit into organizational activities. The primary role of the coach is to ask high-quality, powerful questions that stimulate the client to set their own goals, find their own motivation, keep on track, and revise or assess goals as things come up along the way. The primary role of the client is to be open and committed to the coaching process as a means of personal and professional development.

Some aspects of the coaching contract (the frequency and duration of calls or meetings, the context—whether in person or on the telephone) are set out at the beginning of the coaching relationship and probably won't change. But much of the coach-client dynamic is fluid and adapts as the client grows and changes. This includes the primary focus of the coaching content, the kinds of questions and interventions used by the coach, the degree of accountability, and how the coach can best serve the client.

What has worked in the past might not work in the current situation. The coach and client together evaluate and adjust what they are doing and how it is affecting the progress of the client. Periodic adjustments to the contracted relationship are discussed to make the coaching more powerful. Successful coaching is truly a collaborative process and the client contributes as much as does the coach. The coach contract is a result of working out these relationship dynamics in a conscious manner.

Coaching questions for creating the contract:

Initially —

- How do you want to use me as your coach?
- Tell me what you know about how you get motivated to take action.
- What help do you need to move more quickly toward your goals?

THE COACHING RELATIONSHIP

START

Foundation (intake)
Agreement
Present State
Evaluation
Values
Current Resources
Intent for Coaching

Completion or
Termination
of Coaching,
Backtrack of Coaching,
What Worked,
What Didn't,
Next Steps

Designing the Alliance
Time, Length and
Frequency, Meetings,
Person, Phone, E-mail/Fax
Contract for Behavior,
Ongoing Design
Requests.

Periodic Reviews
Redesign, Celebration,
Letting Go,
Examination of Intent,
Completion

Coaching Sessions
Pre session Rapport,
Directionalizing,
Holding the Space,
What's Called for?
Action/Movement,
Closure, Follow Up

- Do you want me to hold you accountable to take action?
- Do you want in-between assignments?

Ongoing —

- What is working?
- What might we want to change?

COACHING CYCLES

Unlike therapy or some forms of consulting, the coaching agreement typically specifies time parameters for the coaching relationship. These parameters, or coaching cycles, require the coach and client to review the coaching relationship and adjust or discontinue the relationship depending on results and client needs. This is especially helpful when coaching employees because it gives the employee the opportunity to define and manage the coaching relationship.

A common coaching cycle is three months. Three months is long enough to allow the coach and client to develop a powerful coaching relationship but short enough to keep coaching focused. At the end of the cycle, the coach and client hold a review session.

This session allows both parties to:

- Assess the client's progress towards agreed goals.
- Review accomplishments.
- Backtrack or review highlights of the coaching process.
- Revisit the client's values and, if appropriate, life as a whole, to put coaching into perspective.
- Determine whether or not to continue for another cycle of coaching.

If continuing:

- Re-contract for additional three month cycle.
- Monitor and adjust the coaching relationship.
- Identify what has worked and what might need adjusting in the coaching process.
- Determine whether or not to change the primary focus.

If closing

- Get feedback from client about yourself as a coach.
- Determine the next steps for the client.
- If the coach is independent of the company: get a testimonial from client (if willing and appropriate) and get referrals from client.

INTAKE

The intake or foundation meeting is your opportunity to discover what is important to the client and how you can serve her as a coach. The value of taking time with the intake meeting cannot be overstated. This meeting allows you to define your role as a coach and to co-create the coaching relationship. As a professional, you should be clear about the ground rules in the coaching relationship, what you expect from the client, and what the client can count on from you. Discuss confidentiality and the ethics and standards that guide your behavior.

Coaching is not a packaged service or product but a relationship that is unique to each client. The two of you will tailor an alliance that is intended to serve the client. Invite him to make requests and ask for changes in the ongoing coaching relationship, even if a company is paying the bill.

Your first meeting with a client is an "intake meeting". The intake meeting differs from later coaching in that you (the coach) will be setting the agenda for the appointment. You may have written work that the client will do before or during the intake appointment. You will decide what information you want from the client and how to use the time.

Decide how long the session will be. Typical intake appointments are one-and-a-half to two hours. Whatever you decide for your overall time frame, get clear about how much time you will allot to each part. Remember that this a map, a plan, and that few if any appointments will follow the plan exactly.

Schedule an intake with yourself and fine-tune your timing, your "script," and your intake packet. Then you'll be ready to call friends, acquaintances, and other contacts and invite them to hire you as their coach!

Why use an intake meeting?

- To establish a coaching relationship and create a coaching contract with employees, colleagues, or coworkers.
- To provide the foundation for effective coaching.

What does it do?

- Defines the role of the coach and the client. Establishes the structure for the coaching process.
- Provides opportunity to explore the client's strengths, talents, and values.
- Defines the initial goals or the primary focus of the coaching process.

How do I do it?

Set up a meeting to begin the coaching relationship. This meeting should allow enough time to cover the following topics:

- Define the coaching relationship.

- If the coach has a dual relationship with the client (such as a manager coaching an employee), determine how the manager-coach will "switch hats" with the employee.

- Discover the client's strengths, talents, and values.

- Identify the client's overall goals.

- Pick one to three goals to use as a primary focus for the coaching.

- Determine how the client wants to use you as a coach.

- Decide how the client will be held accountable.

What makes coaching different from managing is that the manager-coach and client-employee co-create the coaching relationship. The manager must switch from a "manager hat" to a "coach hat" and enter into a relationship with the employee as a "client." This means that the employee takes the lead in determining the direction and course of the coaching content. In other words, the goals are defined by the client and not by the manager.

To coach effectively as a manager:

- Define the coaching relationship (see the section on The Coach Contract). This step defines roles, clarifies expectations, and provides an opportunity to design the alliance that you will have with the client.

- Determine how the manager-coach will switch hats. This step is necessary when the manager is also a supervisor of the employee. This means that the manager cannot truly function as a coach in the purest sense of the word (see the section on The Coach-Client Relationship). The manager needs to define clear markers for each role, which might include sitting in different chairs or using different rooms for each function. One way to do this is use the metaphor of a hat. The manager tells the client when she is functioning as a manager by "putting on the manager hat" and when she is functioning as a coach by "putting on the coaching hat."

- Discover **the client's strengths, talents, and values.** This is where you get to know the client, learn what is important, and what motivates him. It is worth the time to spend thirty minutes to an hour on this part of the intake. This will allow the client to shine and give you lots of valuable information you can use in coaching him successfully.

  - **Traits:** Ask the client to prepare in advance a list of what he perceives as his personal strengths. This can include qualities and traits, special abilities and skills or other personal assets. Go over the list with him and encourage him to expand on it.

  - **Values:** Ask the client what is important to him, both in general and in relation to work. A simple way to do this is to ask: What do you want in a job? What is important to you in your career? Go through these values and ask how he knows when he is fulfilled.

  - **The Wheel At Work:** Have the client create a picture of the major roles and functions that he fulfills on the job and to determine how well he performs in each area. This is purely a self-assessment and can be useful in helping the client to develop a well-balanced skill set.

  - **Motivation:** An excellent tool at this point is the Meta Program assessment (see the section on Meta Programs).

- **Identify the client's overall goals.** Ask the client to describe long and short-term goals for career and personal development.

- **Career:** What are the client's long-term career goals? Where would she like to be in five years? In ten years? What are the client's more immediate goals within the company? What are her ambitions?

- **Personal development:** What skills and abilities would the client like to develop? What personal qualities or traits would he want to cultivate? What leaders or others might serve as role models or mentors to him?

- **Ask the client to pick one to three goals** to use as a primary focus for the coaching process.

- Determine how the client wants to use you as a coach. Ask the client what she wants in you as a coach and how she would know that the coaching is working. This provides guidelines for the coach to use when coaching the client. Coaching is an evolving process, and the question should be revisited periodically.

- Determine the client wants to be held accountable.

SWITCHING HATS

One of the keys to success as a supervisor-coach is flexibility. It is useful to be able to switch your role and your relationship with your employees to suit specific situations and to get the best results. The downside of flexibility is the perception that the manager is inconsistent. One way to manage this impression is to let people know that you are switching roles and, if appropriate, explain why you are switching roles.

On several occasions, we've mentioned the importance of "switching hats" for those in a manager-coach role. As the idiom goes, a supervisor "wears many hats." You can use this common understanding (at least among English-speaking people) to let your employees know what role you are playing and when you are switching roles. Two basic roles are "manager" and "coach." A simple way to distinguish these roles is as follows:

PURPOSE:

- To maintain clarity of roles.
- To model a method for managing changing roles in a relationships.
- To anchor and access role states and resources.

METHOD:

- Tell the person you are switching roles.
- Act as if you are removing one hat and putting on another.
- Change physiology to match each role.
- If possible and appropriate, use a separate chair or location for each role.

THE UNIVERSAL CYCLES OF CHANGE

What is it?

One way to think about coaching is that it is to help the client manage the change in his or her life in a conscious way. The Universal Cycles of Change is a description of change developed primarily by Kristine Hallbom. It is an incredibly useful model for recognizing that change is not only inevitable and impossible to avoid, it has predictable cycles. If change is not considered or managed, as far as is possible, it will still happen, but typically in a more chaotic way. One of the great things about coaching is this: good coaching will facilitate more positive change and a smoother experience.

Why use it?

- To educate yourself and your client on the nature of change.

- To assess where the client is in the cycles of change.

- To help the client recognize that change is inevitable and has an identifiable structure.

- To help the client manage change effectively through maintaining the awareness of change

What does it do?

- Identifies steps in the change process.

- Offers a "diagnostic" and predictive tool for gauging client status in the change process.

How do I use it?

The Universal Cycles of Change provide a big frame for coaching. By recognizing that change will occur and respecting the cycles of change, you can coach someone to help them move through their lives in a better way. Here is a full description:

The Universal Cycles of Change is an ongoing process that's been happening in our universe for about 13.5 billion years, so it is a really old model. We have observed seven Universal Cycles of Change that occur in all living systems such as plants, trees, stars, cells, and animals. You can also see these same cycles occurring in most nonliving systems such as cars, houses, computers, and the economy.

The Universal Cycles of Change can also be found within all aspects of human life and behavior. They happen in marriages, in business, with health, with families, with various states of mind and so on. We go through these cycles every day and every year of our life. Being aware of these cycles can help us to consciously create the kinds of life experiences that we want, and to bring forth the reality of our choice. The people who do well in life are naturally attuned to these cycles of change.

Here is a description of the seven phases of the Universal Cycles of Change:

Creation. This cycle is about new beginnings. Everything has a starting point, and typically that point begins with an idea, an action, or a blueprint. Some examples of this include starting a business, having a baby, investing in your first stock or fund, creating an idea for a book or a painting, building your first house, getting married, buying a new car, planting the seeds for a vegetable garden, or the Big Bang (the beginning of our universe as we know it).

Growth. When a system begins to grow and develop, it also becomes "self-organizing." What this means is that the initial creation begins to take shape or form. New patterns of behavior start to develop, and the system self-organizes itself around the original creation. For example, a new business develops a wonderful marketing plan, the stock that you've invested in begins to rise in price, the small tree that you've planted shows signs of growth, you install fancy hubcaps and new seat covers in your car, or your child speaks her first words and takes her first steps.

Complexity to Maturity. As a system begins to take shape and form through continued growth, it becomes more complex, to the point where it reaches a "steady state." A system operates at its best when it is in a steady state. Some examples of a steady state are when things are going well in your job, when an athlete "enters into the zone", when the tree that you have planted is sprouting beautiful green leaves, when your marriage is going well, the car that you bought is running great, the stock that you have invested in has made a big jump in the right direction, or when you're feeling good about yourself and everything in your life.

Turbulence–Feedback. When the system becomes too complex in its growth and development, problems begin to develop and turbulence sets in. Turbulence is considered feedback from the environment that the system's complex state can no longer be supported—and that something has to be reorganized, changed, or dropped off. For example, you may have hired someone to work for you who isn't working out, you may start noticing some serious communication problems in your marriage that are affecting your individual health and well–being, the leaves on the tree that you planted begin to change color, you may have invested in a stock that begins to drop, you develop a minor physical symptom that is distracting, you notice signs of depression or dissatisfaction in your life, or your car starts making funny sounds.

Chaos. This is when the system completely falls apart and chaos sets in. For example, the leaves on the tree turn brown and shrivel up, the troublesome employee acts out to the point where the overall welfare of the business is threatened, the stock that you bought takes a huge drop, your marriage is completely falling apart, you get seriously ill, or the funny sound that your car was making turns into a loud choking sound and grey-blue smoke starts blowing out the tail pipe.

"Droppings Off" and Reorganization. Sometimes life becomes so complex that chaos sets in and you have to "drop off" something to help the system regain its overall balance. For example, when the snake sheds its skin or the leaves drop off the tree—these are considered to be droppings off. Even having to replace a part on your car is a form of dropping off or reorganization. In order to move forward through a difficult life challenge you often need to let go of a limiting belief, a dysfunctional relationship, a behavior, or it would open to make space in your life to create something wonderfully new. All life forms in this universe such as trees, snakes, and even stars allow for this natural dropping-off cycle to occur; so do non-living forms, such as computers with trash bins. The purpose of the trash bin is to get rid of extra information on the hard drive because it takes up too much space. Human beings are the only ones that resist these natural cycles of change.

Meditation and Dormancy. The way a system regains its balance is to drop something off. Then it can rejuvenate itself during the dormancy phase, thus allowing itself to recycle back up to a new evolutionary level of creation. Just as the tree stands without leaves in the brisk cold winter, we sometimes need to go into a place of meditation and inner silence. It might be uncomfortable for a while, but it can be very healing to quiet one's mind or to lay low for a while.

Before you can move forward, you need to give yourself plenty of being time to renew and rejuvenate. Once you've done this, you can become creative again. You will have dropped off what was holding you back. Yet you'll still have all the knowledge and wisdom that was gained from the whole experience. This sets the tone for a whole new cycle of creativity and growth. This is the final cycle in which the system regains its balance, which will allow it to recycle back up into…Creation.

The system now has less mass, yet more energy, because it contains all the learnings from the previous cycles. Everything in our universe evolves and grows, and has been doing so for billions of years. Part of this natural evolutionary process includes going through different states of change. Let's consider a tree, since it is a familiar example of the Universal Cycles of Change.

The first cycle that a tree goes through is that of creation, which happens when a seed gets planted. Then the tree grows—given that it has been provided with enough water and sunshine to grow. Over time the tree reaches a steady state of maturity in which all of its leaves have developed with complete beauty.

Then the autumn season sets in; the leaves begin to change color. They turn brown and drop off to the ground. After this happens, the tree stands in dormancy without any leaves. But then spring comes around, the tree sprouts new leaves and the whole process of creation happens again.

Because all living systems get too complex in their growth and development, they must have some kind of a dropping off to regain their balance. Trees do this all the time with their leaves.

We can learn a lot by modeling trees. Have you ever been walking by a tree and its leaves are falling off. And all of a sudden you hear the tree crying out, "Pleeeease, don't let my leaves fall off!" This never happens. The tree has mastered the art of dropping off and recycling back up to creation. Snakes are the same way when they shed their skin. I have never known of a snake to resist the process. Even most computers have trash bins to drop off the excess information that can slow down their hard drive, which thus allows for the computer to operate more quickly and creatively.

Interestingly, there is only one living system that does not allow it to naturally go through this 15-billion-year-old process of change. This same system allows itself to stay stuck in turbulence and chaos for extended periods of time. This same system often resists dropping off what needs to be dropped off. Can you guess which system it is? Human beings, of course.

People represent the only living systems that will allow themselves to stay stuck in turbulence and chaos. They are the only living systems that will not drop off whatever needs to be dropped off in their life. We see this resistance happening a lot in relationships, career, and health.

One man shared an amazing realization that he had about the Universal Cycles of Change and how they related to him. This man had a teenage daughter with whom he had been unable to communicate effectively or happily for several years. After learning about the universal cycles of change, he said,

> "I finally understand why I have been having so many problems with my 17 year old daughter. In my mind I still think of her as a little child. I am now realizing that I need to 'drop off' my perception of her as a child and start treating her like a young adult. It makes complete sense to me why there has been so much turbulence and chaos in our relationship over the last couple of years."

In the case of the man who was having problems with his teenage daughter, it's not like he could just "drop off" the relationship with his child. His only option was to reorganize who he was within the context of the relationship. As soon as he stopped treating her like a little girl, and started treating her like an adult, their relationship got better.

The magic in what he did with his daughter can be found within the structure of his internal experience. He had an internal representation of her being a little girl. When he shifted that representation to her being an adult, then she started acting like an adult. By doing this, he was able to create an entirely new experience with his daughter.

An English woman described a powerful experience that she had with her children and the Universal Cycles of Change model. She said, "I just have to tell you about the funniest thing that happened to me last night. After I learned the Universal Cycles of Change model, I made the decision that I needed to 'drop off' the co-dependent relationship that I have with my five adult children," she said with excitement.

She continued:

"Even though my children are grown up, they are all so needy. I felt like my life was all about them and there was no room for me. On my drive home last night, I set the intent to release the co-dependence that has been keeping me enmeshed with my children for so many years.

THE UNIVERSAL CYCLES OF CHANGE

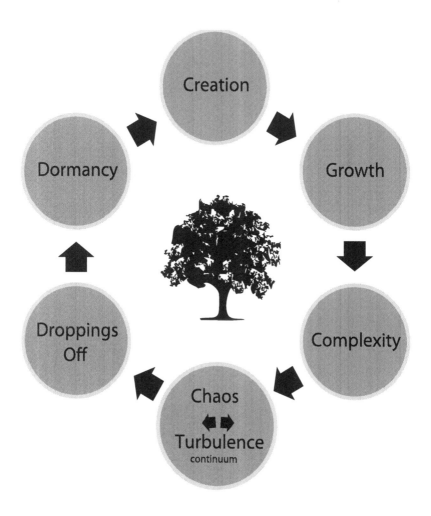

After I got home, all 'chaos' broke loose. One by one, each child phoned me with some major crisis. One of my children's cars broke down, another had just broken up with a boyfriend, another was having a bad day, and so on. The phone just kept ringing off the hook with their problems. I told each child one by one that they were responsible for themselves from now on and that they will need to solve their own problems," she said.

At this point in the story, she was glowing as she continued "I just wanted to tell you that today is the beginning of the rest of my life. I am no longer co-dependent with my children and I can have my life back! I am going to go back to school and I am also going to start painting again, and doing the kinds of things that make me happy. I am going to start living my life for me now, instead of for everyone else."

So often people are afraid to make changes, because they are worried about throwing their lives into turbulence and chaos. In the case of the English woman, she was worried that her grown children would feel resentment towards her if she were not always fully present for them. Instead of being present for her children, she ended up resenting them because she wasn't getting to live the life she wanted. Once she released her children from the bonds of co-dependent enmeshment, she was able to evolve into a new way of interacting with them. And in doing so, she found that she could be more present for her children because she felt more spiritually fulfilled in her life.

As mentioned earlier, the Universal Cycles of Change influence all the areas of our lives. The primary life areas that they affect are:

LIFE WHEEL

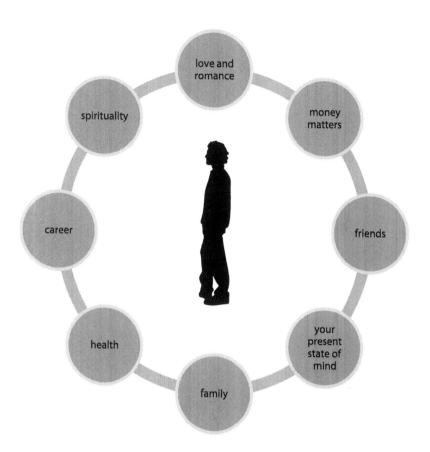

When you assess each area of your life, which universal cycle of change are you experiencing in that context? If any of your areas are in turbulence or chaos, you may want to ask yourself,

"What are some things that I need to drop off so that I can bring my life back into balance?"

It doesn't always have to be a dramatic dropping off. You can drop off something as simple as reading the morning newspaper or drinking diet coke every day. Some other examples of things that may need to be dropped off are: behaviors, beliefs, attitudes, ways of thinking, perceptions, habits, jobs, and relationships. Other examples might include: smoking, drinking too much alcohol, weight, television, coffee, unclear boundaries, frenetic busyness, old relationships that need to be updated, a troublesome employee, a toxic friendship, clutter, disorganization, grudges, anger, jealousy, unnecessary debt, and unfinished business with people.

Our outer reality is a reflection of our inner reality. What nature can do for us is to serve as a perfect model for creating the life we want, as well as evolving to higher levels of personal and spiritual fulfillment. The answers to creating what we want in life can be found by becoming aware of the Universal Cycles of Change and applying them to all the various life areas. There is no reason why we can't harness the same kind of creative potential that exists within the seed of a plant or a star in our galaxy.

Barbara Walters was interviewing multi-billionaire Bill Gates, and asked him, "Now that you're the richest man in the world and you can have anything you desire, what more could you possibly want?" Gates replied, "To never stop changing. Whatever I do today will be considered history tomorrow. I have to make sure that I never stop creating, and that I am always changing."

Suggested Reading: *A Brief History of Everything,* by Ken Wilber; *Complexity,* by M. Mitchell Waldrop; *The Web of Life,* by Fritjof Capra; *The Tree of Knowledge,* by Humberto Maturana and Francisco Varela; *Chaos: Making A New Science,* by James Gleick; *Steps to an Ecology of Mind,* by Gregory Bateson; and *Psycho–Cybernetics, by Maxwell Maltz.*

META PROGRAMS

Meta Programs are subconscious mental-emotional filters that determine what you attend to, what you sort for, and what you respond to in life. These patterns identify how you process information and what motivates you to act. Meta Program profiling is especially helpful for coaching employees because Meta Programs also directly apply to the work situation.

These filters form your communication style and your preferences for how you interact with others and the world. Identifying your client's Meta Programs provides a "profile" of the client's working style and motivational patterns. Once you know your client's Meta Programs, you can tailor the coaching process to their unique ways and maximize the coaching impact.

The Meta Programs as described below are adapted from the work of Roger Bailey as well as from the work of Richard Bandler and Leslie Cameron-Bandler. (Rodger Bailey is currently making exciting new discoveries about linguistic patterns and Meta Programs. He can be reached at http://www.labprofile.com) For a full description of Meta Programs, see the book, *Words that Change Minds,* by Shelley Rose Charvet.

It is important to note that these patterns are contextual. S/he can and will be somewhat different for different contexts in life. In other words, the set of Meta Programs that you use for work may be different from the set used for relationships. Therefore, it is important to hold one context in mind when considering Meta Programs.

Why use it?

- To determine someone's thinking style.

- To learn what motivates others.

- To tailor your communication style to the client's style of processing input.

- To deliver effective coaching assignments and encourage client action toward goals.

What does it do?

- Helps you to get to know your client.

- Provides questions to "profile" another person's thinking and motivation style.

- Gives information to improve communication effectiveness.

- Gives you, as manager-coach, the ability to make accurate predictions of how the client is likely to perform in specific contexts.

- Gives you a way to identify what will motivate and demotivate your client.

How do I do it?

You can use the Meta Program profile in your intake interview. Explain that the profile serves as a tool for understanding your client and an aid in providing tailored coaching services. Many of the individual Meta Program questions can also be asked as stand-alone questions at any time during the coaching process or to gather information about a context that is different than the one used in the intake. For instance, if the intake context is the job, you may ask later using the context of co-worker relationships.

PART 1: PROCESS

First, we will consider an overview of how to use the tool. This will include the general steps to follow throughout the questioning process. Then, we will analyze the specific items in the profile.

General process:

1. Establish the context for the questions, such as job/career, or co-worker relationships. You will need to insert references to the context for certain questions and should make sure the client keeps the same context in mind throughout the interview.

2. Ask the questions using the exact words with addition of references to the context where appropriate. The questions have been carefully designed to get specific types of response. If you vary the wording, you may contaminate the responses and get invalid information.

3. Listen carefully to the client's responses. In some cases, you are listening for the form of the response in addition to the content. This means that you are attending to how the person responds (non-verbal patterns, tone of voice, etc.) as well as the sequencing of the response.

4. Some items offer a checklist for potential responses. Use the checklist to designate the client's style based on the response.

5. In some cases, you will note the exact key words/phrases used by the client. Make sure you use the client's key words and not synonyms or substitutes for them.

6. Keep in mind that most of the Meta Programs operate on a continuum. Virtually no one is all one way or another. Most people will skew to one side or the other. Meta Programs do not place someone in a category; s/he instead reveals unconscious predictive drives and preferences.

7. With practice, you can complete a Meta Program interview with someone conversationally and be able to make very accurate predictions about what environment, job, relationship, etc., will offer the greatest chances for success.

PART 2: ITEM ANALYSIS

Please look at the interviews form on pages 47-48. Keep in mind that all people have all traits.

Criteria

Criteria words are the words that a person (client) uses to describe what s/he considers to be important in a particular situation. These words are very meaningful to the client and elicit a strong feeling response. It is vital to recognize that the client's exact words are the ones to use. These words are deeply anchored to his/her experience, whereas synonyms may not be. It is helpful to get five or six criteria words. Some of them will be very important to the client.

For example, a client that we worked with had "top pay" as an important criterion in his work. When the words "top pay" were used in communicating with him, he lit up and became very attentive. Any other synonyms, such as "good money," "high commission," "large remuneration," etc. were greeted with wariness on his part.

☞ Questions:

- What do you want in a (job, task, coach session, etc.)?
- What's important to you in this context?
- How is_____ of value to you?

- When the client answers the questions, write down the criteria words he/she uses. Feed them back and notice the positive response you get.

We use specific measures to determine if our criteria are met. For instance, if a criteria word for the context of a job is "challenge," then the person will sort for particular kinds of experiences judged as "challenging." One person may find an assignment requiring development of new procedures "challenging," while another may find it "challenging" to negotiate between people.

- How do you know when (name his/her criteria) is met?
- What has to happen for (name his/her criteria) to be fulfilled for you?
- When the client answers the questions, write down the response he/she gives, and you'll begin to understand what the client needs to feel motivated and interested.

MOTIVATION TO TAKE ACTION

Are you motivated *toward* goals that you want to attain, or does a*voiding potential negative consequences* motivate you? Or some combination of both?

Toward: You are motivated to achieve or attain goals. You have trouble recognizing problems. You are good at managing priorities.

Away from: You focus on what could go wrong, and what is going wrong now. You are motivated to fix problems and have trouble keeping focused on what you want to achieve.

- What does having that (name the client's criteria) do for you?

- What's important about that (name the client's criteria?)?

- What's in it for you?

Responses indicating a "toward" response: reach goal; obtain; have; get; achieve; reward.

Responses indicating an "away from" response: avoid; steer clear of; not have; get rid of; exclude; away from.

You'll hear both kinds of words if the person has a mixed response. You will want to use the balance of "toward" and "away from" words when trying to help the client get motivated.

DECISION SOURCE: "WHO DECIDES, ME OR SOMEONE ELSE?"

Internal: You are self-motivated in the chosen context; you might have difficulty accepting other's opinions and direction in a certain context. You "know best." When feedback is given, you might question the person giving it. You gather information and decide upon its usefulness. You know when you've done something well or not as a kind of inner certainty. You have a strong inner conviction about the right action to take. You might be hard to manage as you may not take direction well.

External: You want, and in fact, require, other people's ideas, opinions, and feedback about how you are doing or what to do. You don't have clear inner standards for the best action to take. Unless you receive feedback from an external source, you might feel lost. You are likely to receive a suggestion as a command.

- How do you know that you've done a good job?

Internally referenced people will tell you they see it done properly, or "it just feels right," or "I know," or words to that effect. Externally referenced people will mention some kind of feedback from others. People who are both internal and external will mention both an inner knowing as well as external feedback.

Appropriate language to use for understanding and rapport:

Internal: What do you think? "You're the only one to decide; please consider; it's up to you; here's information so you can decide..."

External: Everyone knows... "You'll get helpful feedback; this is well-respected information; it has been approved by; experts say..."

PROCEDURES VS. OPTIONS

☞ **Question:**

- Do you need to create new ways to do things or do you prefer to follow established procedures?

Procedures: You prefer to have rules or procedures to follow. You believe that there is a "right way" to do things in many situations. When you have no procedure to follow, you have no starting place. You might bumble around, not being clear on what to do. If you are a "procedures person," you will follow the recipe instead of inventing your own way. **Note:** Often people follow procedures when learning something new, then expand to find new ways of doing things.

Options: If you have the options Meta Program, you'll want to develop new ways of doing things. To you, every situation is a new experience that offers a chance for developing a new way to resolve it. You are motivated by what needs to be done, not the way to do it. You are good at creating procedures for others to follow, but might have difficulty following them yourself. You will tend to break the rules. For example, you will not typically assemble something by following the instructions, but will do it your own way.

☞ Question:

- "Why did you choose your present (name context)_____?"

Options people will give criteria. Procedures people will tell a story about how they got the job. Someone who is a mix of the two will give criteria and tell a story.

Appropriate language to use for understanding and rapport:

With "procedural" clients: Speak in ordinals ("Do this first, then that second, etc."); we need to do it the right way; steps to take. Talk to them using the procedures s/he can use. For example, notice the difference in these two statements: "Call Phyllis for information." vs. a more procedural sentence, "Pick up the phone and call Phyllis at (555) 555-5555 and ask how you can receive your free gift now." Talk about the "right way" to do something.

With "optional clients": "Do it your way", talk about what outcome is needed not "how to do it," alternatives; possibilities, new way of doing it, etc.

MODE OF COMPARISON

- Sameness: You look for similarities, for what is the same. You have a very long clock, and dislike change.

- Sameness with Exception: You notice what is the same, and then you will identify exceptions. You'll need a significant change every seven years.

- Difference: You notice what is different. You are more likely to mismatch what people say. You need significant change frequently. (In the world of work, you need major changes in your job every 18 months, according to Rodger Bailey.)

☞ Question:

- "What is the relationship between your (context) this year and (context) last year?" (For example, "What is the relationship between your job this year and last year?")

- "Sameness" clients will respond by saying, "It's the same."

- "Sameness-with-exception" clients will say, "It's the same except I am working longer;" "It's better this year;" "I like my boss more;" etc. Listen for words like more, better, improved, less, except, etc.

- "Difference" clients will say, "It is different." Or "It's all new," or other words that speak to differences.

CONVINCER

What type of evidence does a person need to gather in order to start the process of being convinced? This has two parts, "channel" and "mode."

Channel

- **See:** Visual evidence: you need to see the behavior, action or product. (Or you need to see a representation of it, like a diagram or a picture.)

- **Read:** You are convinced because something is in writing. When you have read it, you begin to become convinced.

- **Hear:** You need to be told about something, or hear the buzz about it.

- **Do:** You have to actually do something, or actively do something with another person.

☞ Question:

- How do you know when someone is doing a good job?

Responses will be a version of: "I see it, or heard about it, or I read it, or I tried it out."

Appropriate language to use for understanding and rapport: Match the sensory channel.

Mode

- **Channel Number of Examples:** You need to witness an action, service, skill, or product a certain number of times to be convinced or learn something.

- **Automatic:** You will make assumptions that something is the case with only a little information. You may jump to conclusions or give the benefit of the doubt. Once you have made up your mind, you do not easily change it.

- **Consistent:** You need to reevaluate every time. You are never completely convinced.

- **Period of Time:** You need to gather information over time before you are sure of something.

ACTION LEVEL

Does this person take initiative or wait for others? This may change by context. A person may be proactive in a situation that s/he is familiar with, and reactive in one where it is unclear what action to take, the safety of the situation, etc. For example, one shy client was proactive in situations where he knew all the others involved and knew they liked him. He became reactive in situations dealing with strangers until he thought they felt OK about him. Then he would gradually get more proactive.

Proactive: You take initiative. At the extreme, you "go for it" with little or no planning. You are motivated by taking action, and demotivated if you have to wait. Appropriate language to use for understanding and rapport: do it; go for it; make it happen; now; get it done; don't wait.

Reactive: You wait for others to take action or gather information before moving ahead. You are motivated to bide your time, analyze the situation, "don't fix it if it isn't broken," etc. You will do well in jobs where people come to you and you can react to their needs rather than having to initiate the action. Appropriate language to use for understanding and rapport: evaluate; understand; think about; wait; study; ponder; might; could; would; assess.

☞ **Question:**

There is not a specific question for this pattern—listen to the language used by the client. Proactive people will use words like "go for it, just do it", etc. Reactive people will say works like "wait," or will want to check it out first, etc.

BIG PICTURE VS. DETAIL ORIENTATION

Does the person pay attention to the "big picture" or details—in other words does s/he tend to notice the forest or the trees?

Specific (Focus on the Details): You deal well with small chunks of information and may have trouble summarizing or seeing the bigger picture. You tend to be sequential and linear in your thinking and descriptions. You give lots of information and detail and will expect detailed descriptions from others. You are effective where details must be handled. You can be identified because you give lots of information as you talk about something.

General (Focus on the Big Picture): You tend to think conceptually, and see things in an overview. You will talk in summaries; give one or two word answers, etc. You'll become frustrated if forced to deal with or listen to lots of details for lengthy periods.

☞ **Question:**

- Tell me about a work experience that you really enjoyed.

If the client gives lots of information she is more likely oriented toward detail. If the client gives little information or a broad summary, she is more likely to be a big picture person.

Appropriate language to use for understanding and rapport:

With the Detail oriented person (Specific) "exactly"; "precisely"; "particularly"; "specifically" (and give lots of details in sequence)

With the Big Picture (General) person: "The important thing is; "in general"; "here is the bottom line"; "here is the big picture"; etc.

ATTENTION DIRECTION

☞ **Question:**

- Do you naturally pay attention to the nonverbal behavior of others, or to your own internal experiences?

There is no specific question for this pattern. It can be identified through observation of the client's non-verbal behavior.

Self: You tend not to show your feelings, and may have a flat affect. You tend to be more aware of yourself and your needs than those of others. You pay attention to the words said rather than the nonverbal cues offered by others and may miss some messages people send you. Interpersonal communication skills are not your strong point.

Appropriate language to use for understanding and rapport: Keep the communication focused on content; match criteria.

Other: You respond immediately to other's communications or behaviors and are adept at hearing voice tone shifts and noticing body language. You can't not respond to others. You tend to be more animated.

Appropriate language to use for understanding and rapport: increase the depth of rapport by matching or acknowledging affect.

TIME ORIENTATION

What time reference does the person typically use? The past? The present? The future?

Past-oriented: You are focused on the past. You can access past experiences easily. You can find it difficult to deal with change, and are not good at planning. You may seem critical of new ideas and proposals. ("We tried that five years ago and it didn't work.")

Present oriented: You are oriented now. You feel your feelings clearly. You tend to be "in the moment" and get caught up in what you are doing at any given time. At the extreme, you can get lost in the moment and not consider the past or the future.

Future-oriented: You are good at planning. At the extreme, you might not notice what is happening now, and may not learn from past errors.

Appropriate language to use for understanding and rapport: use the same time references as the client.

STYLE

What kind of environment allows the person to be most productive: working alone, with others around, or sharing responsibility?

Independent: You like to work alone and have responsibility for your results. The quality of your work can suffer if you have to share decisions or work with others as a part of a team.

Proximity: You want to have the responsibility for the project, but like to have others involved or around, "in proximity." Productivity will fall if you have to share responsibility as a member of a team, or if you have to work all by yourself. You are a good project manager.

Cooperative: You like being a part of the team and want to share responsibility with others. You may have trouble with deadlines if you have to work alone. As a manager you will want to do things with your employees.

☞ **Question:**

- Tell me about an experience that was (Criteria) and what did you like about it?

In the response, listen for whether the client just talks about what he did (independent), about himself and others ("I helped my direct report to establish new goals"), or if the client says "We…" or "Us…" etc.

Appropriate language to use for understanding and rapport:

With an Independent client: You will do it yourself; by yourself; you have the responsibility; you'll work independently; you're the one, no one will bother you.

With a Proximity client: You'll be in working with others, but have the ultimate responsibility, you'll be in charge; you are the lead person, etc.

With a Cooperative client: Us; we; all together; teamwork, shared responsibility; let's, etc.

Example: Putting This Idea To Work

Rebecca worked in the HR/training department of a large corporation. HR staff offered some limited coaching services to the managers and employees. She had been coaching Eric, a middle manager, but the coaching was going slowly and Rebecca felt that she was missing something important about Eric. She learned the Meta Program profiling tool and applied it with Eric both to learn the tool and to improve her coaching with him.

Rebecca immediately learned her style of coaching had been mismatching Eric in three ways. First, Eric was very options oriented while Rebecca was procedural. So, she kept asking him questions about specific steps, which Eric seemed to "avoid." She realized he wasn't really avoiding, he just did not think that way. She started using more options language and immediately found that Eric responded more positively.

Second, Eric's working style was "cooperative," and he needed to work with others. She had missed this about him and found Erik had failed to follow through on her suggestions for assignments. She realized that she had been giving him individual assignments, primarily self-reflective exercises that he could do on his own. She shifted to giving assignments that involved acting with others and found that Erik was more excited about the assignments and more likely to complete them.

Third, she recognized that Eric was motivated by external reasons and knew that he wanted to please her and others. She could see how this had resulted in some problems in the coaching process—Eric wanted answers and she had refused to give them to him. She changed the direction of assignments suggesting he find mentors or read books, external authorities, to help him address specific issues.

Rebecca found many other patterns that served her in coaching Eric more effectively. She found that she could match his criteria and evidence as a powerful tool for understanding his motivation and for coaching him on issues. She also used his pattern of going from general to specific to sequence coaching topics and found the whole process going more smoothly. Overall, she felt she was much more effective with Eric when she matched his style.

META-PROGRAM PROFILE

Name _____

Date _____

Pattern	Question	Response
Criteria	What do you want in a job? What is important to you in a job?	
Evidence	How do you know when your (criteria) is met? What indicates (criteria) is met?	
Direction:	What does having (criteria) met do for you?	☐ Toward ☐ Away
Source	How do you know that you have done a good job?	☐ Internal ☐ External
Reason	Why do you choose your current job?	☐ Options ☐ Procedures
Mode of comparison	What is the relationship between your job this year and last year?	☐ Sameness ☐ Progress ☐ Difference
Convincer Channel	How do you know when a coworker is good at his or her job?	☐ See ☐ Hear ☐ Read ☐ Do

Pattern	Question	Response
Convincer Mode:	How many times do you need to (see, hear, read, do) this in order for you to be convinced?	☐ Once ☐ # of times ☐ Time Period ☐ Every Time
Action Level	(Proactive people use active sentences. Reactive people use passive sentences.)	☐ Proactive ☐ Reactive
Detail vs. Big Picture:	If we were going to work on a project together, what would you need to know?	☐ Specific (small chunk) ☐ General (large chunk) ☐ Sequence
Attention Direction:	No specific question	☐ Self ☐ Other ☐ Comparison
Time Orientation:	No specific question	Past Present Future
Style	Tell me about an experience that was (criteria) and what you like about it.	☐ Sameness ☐ Progress ☐ Difference

Coaching 101: The Basics

COMMUNICATION BLOCKERS

What are they?

These are responses typically intended to be helpful but which often don't work and can actually discourage good communications. One of the biggest challenges facing the manager-coach, or HR/EA coach, is overcoming the tendency to direct the employee, which often occurs through these communication blockers. Thomas Gordon (the developer of Leader Effectiveness Training, 1977) lists sixteen such responses, which follow below.

Why do it?

Exploring these common communication mistakes will sensitize you to them and help make you more conscious of them so you can avoid them.

How do I do it?

The goal is to sensitize you to the problem state. All of us slip into these problem communications occasionally. Imagine how you would feel if you were a client and getting responses like these:

Solution Giving: "Here is what you need to do to solve your problem."

Commanding: "Just stop talking so that I can give you my opinion!"

Warning: "If you miss another session, I won't work with you as a coach."

Moralizing: "You should be more gentle with yourself; being critical of yourself or others is not very useful."

Lecturing: "Research shows that a state of uncertainty is helpful to learning new things in a coach context."

Advising: "Why don't you go and talk directly to the person that you are having trouble with.? Getting it out in the open will help you to feel better."

Judgments: "I don't think that what you are planning to do is a good idea."

Blaming: "There's no one to blame but you for the problem you're having, is there?"

Name calling: "I agree with you that your boss sounds like a complete idiot."

Analyzing: "I'm sure I was quite clear. Perhaps we should work on your listening skills."

Denying: "Your boss isn't angry with you, it's just the way he comes across."

Praising: "Good boy for making an attempt to understand it. Trying is the important thing."

Reassuring: "You poor old thing. Hang in there, though. Life's bound get easier over time."

Distracting: "Maybe we should change the subject so that we can get some distance from the problem."

Interrogating: "What were you doing when it happened?" "Why weren't the other staff members involved?" "What did your assistant do?"

Questioning the client's judgment: "Do you always have trouble with that employee?" "Is there something else that you could do to communicate with him?" "Have you tried a number of different ways to get through to him?" "Is he having personal problems that you don't know about?"

It can be helpful for the manager as coach to recognize which of these communication blockers he or she might be in the habit of using and to avoid them. None of them has a place in coaching, and will most likely have the opposite effect from "bringing out the best in the client."

COACHING AND NONVERBAL COMMUNICATION

Why use it?

To dramatically improve your communications and have more conscious control over your own internal experience.

What is it?

We are always a part of a system. You are a system made up of a number of other systems: you have a circulatory system, a digestive system, a musculoskeletal system, a nervous system, and so on. Whenever one of these systems is impacted, the relationships between all of the systems shift. For example, when you alter your posture in certain ways, you will change the way that you see, hear, and come across to others.

How do I do it?

Nonverbal communication is highly significant in overall communication. To really understand this, try the following experiment.

- Scoot back on your chair so that your posterior is touching the back of the chair and you are sitting upright. Lean forward slightly and imagine that you are in a conversation with someone. Notice your state. Now, scoot forward in your chair about six inches, then sit back and rest your upper back on the chair. Notice how your state changes. Move back and forth from these two positions, noticing the angle of your vision and what shifts in your consciousness.

- Leaning more forward—more focused, connected. Leaning back—more detached, looking more at the big picture. Notice the change in the angle of your vision.

- Now try this: Stand up with your feet about hip width apart. Notice the angle of your vision. Then move your toes out and heels toward each other slightly. Notice the visual shift; then move your feet so that they are straight (really straight, like railroad tracks) and again, notice the difference in the angle of your vision.

- Now go for a walk, first with your feet straight, then with them open. Check out the difference in your attitude and what you attend to when "straight" versus "open." Most people experience a profound difference. With your feet straight, you are most likely in a state of purposeful attention. When your feet are open, you slow down, look around more, and feel more laid back.

Consider the implications for coaching. As you change your posture, profound communication differences arise in your ability to gain connection and understanding. Keep in mind that one posture or stance is not better than another but that each simply produces a different outcome.

SYSTEMIC COMMUNICATIONS

We have explored how subtle shifts in body posture will create dramatically different experiences in communication and connection. What happens to a system consisting of two people in communication?

Find a colleague and try this process in actual experience: Merely reading about it won't give you the same discoveries as actually doing it, and you will end up with "academic" understanding.

☞ Exercise

In your pair, appoint two roles:

- An employee who is coming to work late.

- A supervisor who gives feedback about this to the employee.

- The employee doesn't respond but notes how she receives the feedback.

☞ Round One: Supervisor gives the feedback "face to face"

When the feedback is given, notice how the supervisor delivers the feedback and how the employee receives it. Explore the distance between supervisor and employee and the angle of the supervisor's feet (straight versus toes turned out). In most Western cultures, people will communicate with each other face to face and about an arm's length apart. Start by giving the feedback from an arm's length away.

The supervisor should experiment by splaying his feet slightly while giving the feedback, then giving it with his feet straight. Notice the response received and the way that it feels to be the supervisor with each of these variations. Now step closer and express the feedback from fifteen inches away. Again, take a moment to notice the feelings and any shifts in tone of voice, selection of words, or other behaviors.

Now move apart by seven or eight feet. Deliver the feedback and note the changes on the part of both people.

Give the feedback about coming to work late while standing at a three-quarters angle from your partner. Notice what shifts in the analogue of the supervisor and employee. (Analogue refers to the voice tone and tempo, body language, muscle tension, and autonomic changes that occur in a communication. In other words, all the signals except content.) Explore the distance. Notice how you can get closer when you are to the side of the employee and how that changes the interaction. Also notice how you can stay more connected when you are farther away.

Now add a touch. Make it a momentary touch on the arm, much as you would as if someone were blocking your way at the supermarket. You might lean over, barely touch her and say, "Excuse me." Pay attention to how your analogue changes with the touch. Note how the employee responds. Years ago, a study on honesty was conducted, and it was found that people tended to be more honest when they were appropriately touched. Of course, touching people does not cause them to be more honest, but touch creates a different relationship. In the supervisor-employee experiment, notice that there will be a softening of the voice and a different countenance on the part of the supervisor.

Last, try giving feedback on the left side of the person, and then deliver it from their right side. Notice the difference in response. Also attend to your feelings as supervisor. The employee is probably looking at you differently from one side or the other.

When we (Tim Hallbom and Suzi Smith, another coach and NLP Trainer) first discovered this, we thought it had to do with handedness or a dominant side. However, our research showed that about half the people prefer feedback on their right side and about half on the left. We discovered that side preference has to do with self-talk. Most people have a critical voice that they hear in their mind that was "installed" while they were growing up. It is an interjected voice that they acquired from Dad or Mom or some other significant person. These critical voices typically seem to come from one side or the other. We don't like criticism that comes from the side on which we criticize ourselves.

The point of these exercises is to notice how profoundly relationships can change by changing the spatial relationship between the listener and the speaker. As a rule, the coach should be "to the side" of the client. Talking straight on is good for an informal chat but not for the serious work of coaching when you want to be unobtrusive and allow the client space to process her thoughts. Try these experiments in "real-life situations," and you will learn some very powerful communication skills.

ACTIVE LISTENING AND BACKTRACKING

What is it?

Great coaches are highly effective listeners. Developing a good ability to feedback what you are hearing is a key listening skill. "Backtracking" is a special kind of active listening where the coach is feeding back what clients say to you using their key words. When you use the client's own words you will be communicating in the same way that they are thinking.

Why use it?

Backtracking is useful for:

1. Gaining rapport through matching the content and the process words of the client's statements.

2. Making sure you understand the client's statements.

3. Giving you time to think about what you're going to say next.

4. Forcing you to really listen to what the client is saying so you can repeat parts of it back.

5. Letting the client know you are really listening.

6. Observing client commitment, watch for a congruent "whole body yes" to statements that you backtrack. It will tell you the client's level of genuine commitment. For example, when the client says, "I want X." Coach responds, "Oh, so you want X." Watch for a clear congruent "Yes!"

How to do it:

Listen attentively. Feed back what the client says, being sure to use their process words (predicates.)

☞ **Example (key words are italicized):**

- Client: "I am worried about my role in the XYZ project."

    - Coach: "So you're *worried about your role in the XYZ project.* What is it specifically that concerns you?"

- Client: "I am not really clear about how much authority I have for making spending decisions."

    - Coach: "So you are needing to know about *how much authority you have...*"

- Client: "Yes. I get really stuck when I worry about making decisions that my boss won't later support."

    - Coach: " So what can you do to work with her so that you don't get *stuck* in this way?"

And so on.

PERCEPTUAL POSITIONS

What is it?

A key element of many coaching processes is helping the client take a new perspective. These perspectives are actually different perceptual positions and different ways of thinking. This process is especially helpful in coaching employees because work requires cooperative effort and the ability to shift between all three of the perceptual position when appropriate.

There are three perceptual positions: Self, Other, and Observer:

Self: When you're writing in "first person," you use the pronoun I—"I woke up that morning, and I went to school." That's writing from "Self." It is also an associated position. In this position, you're in your body, you're hearing and seeing things through your own experience, and you are accessing your own neurology. It's your point of view, which is, of course, colored by all your unique beliefs, attitudes, experiences, limitations, and knowledge.

Other: In this position, you are considering a situation as if you were the other person—looking at it through their eyes, adopting their physiology, personal values, and personal history (as far as you are informed). The more complete the shift, the more information you'll gather. It's like saying, "If I were you, how would I think about this?" You "become" another person and take on his perspective.

Observer: In this position, you are considering a situation from a neutral, third-party point of view, seeing yourself and the others involved. This is an objective point of view, and you take the detached, disassociated perspective. In this position, you use the pronouns "she," "he," and "they." You are "going meta" to the situation—you're stepping back from it. You're no longer in it but are the observer of it, and you only have the feelings of the observer.

When you step back from Self and consider "the big picture" of something, you are in more of an Observer position. Sometimes we call this a "meta-position." It's not being in an experience; it's stepping back from it and considering it.

Imagine that you're going to go parachuting. Initially, you are in the position on the ground, watching the airplane go by and watching people jump out of an airplane. After they fall for a little bit, the parachute opens, and you see them float down. You can imagine seeing someone who looks like you doing that. Try that in your mind, and notice what that feels like.

Now imagine that you're actually in the airplane. You're flying along, the doors open, you're looking out, and you can feel the breeze blowing. There are a few people ahead of you, and you watch them jump out of the plane. Then it's your turn. You look way down to the ground, twelve thousand feet below. You can hear the sound of the motors and feel the vibration of the airplane. Then you jump out. You begin to fall! You reach out and pull the cord—you feel the parachute open, catch you, and stop you for a second, and you float down to the ground.

The first narrative describes the "observer position;" the second one, the "self" position. What's the difference in your experience? In the first story, there's not much feeling. You only have the detached, objective feelings of the Observer, not those of the participant (Self).

People remember events from different perspectives. Take a minute and think of some positive experience that you've had in the last few months. It could have been something important that you did with someone else, a personal success at work, or a fun evening that you spent with a friend. How do you remember it? You may remember it by being in it, looking out of your own eyes. You might remember it from the perspective of "watching yourself." You may even flip back and forth between viewpoints.

Now think of a negative experience that happened in the last few months. Don't choose the worst event of your life; recall a minor event such as when someone was rude to you or you lost something. Notice how you think about it. How do you recall that negative experience? From an associated or disassociated state? From a disassociated place, you'll likely think, "That happened, but it's in the past." If you remember it from an associated state, you will be stepping back into those negative feelings all over again.

Do you know people who are always negative, grouchy, unfriendly or depressed? They may be continually accessing their negative experiences from the Self position instead of from Observer.

It's useful to start noticing these perspectives and realize that you have a choice about them. When you're in Self, you're going to have access to your passion and your feelings. When you're in the Observer position, you're going to be detached. They're both useful positions for different situations.

Exceptional actors often go to the Other position with their character and mentally become the character. A great example of perceptual positions is the work of actor Dustin Hoffman. When he starred in the film "Rain Man", he played an autistic savant. He created the character from several sources but in particular by studying a man named Kim Peek, who has been referred to as the "real Rain Man." Peek had some remarkable abilities, as is depicted in the film. Hoffman studied him for hours. He learned how to "go Other" with Kim Peek so precisely that he moved and sounded just like him.

About fifteen years ago, a psychological association tried to pass a law that basically proposed "only psychologists could do psychological interventions to effect change with other people." The legislative bill stated that psychology consists of anything you do that induces change in anyone else, whether you get paid for it or not. Certain professions were exempt, such as teachers, clergy, licensed social workers, psychiatrists, and doctors, but if you think about it, the bill could impact training, managing, swimming instruction, or anything. For example, if you go to training, you're learning new skills. Imagine that you went to a Spanish class and just as you said, "Hola, que tal?" the police could nab your instructors and throw them into jail.

What perceptual position had the association taken? It was looking at "psychology" only from its point of view; it never considered all the other points of view. One of the larger groups that strongly opposed the bill was a program for the elderly, which was completely staffed by volunteers. They weren't licensed therapists, they were all volunteers, but the bill would have shut down all those programs for senior citizens in the state. Fortunately, the bill didn't pass.

This is an example of looking at an issue from only one perspective. Wise decision-making involves inclusion of various perspectives. Passionate commitment is one thing, wisdom is another. Vincent van Gogh was passionate about his painting and excelled in his art. On the other hand, he didn't have wisdom: it probably wasn't wise to chop off his ear and give it to someone as a pick-up line.

Gandhi was once asked how he thought he could negotiate with England. He didn't have any money or power, compared to the huge government that controlled his country. Gandhi said, "First, I'm going to consider the negotiation from the point of view of truth." Gandhi was a person who devoted his life to finding his truth (his autobiography is called *My Experiments with Truth*). He was trying to find out what was true in the world and how to learn from that space. Where would his truth be? It would originate in his Self perspective.

Gandhi said, "I'm going to consider truth from the point of view of the Viceroy, the Untouchables, the Hindus, and the Muslims." A woman who lived in the ashram with him said that before the negotiation with the Viceroy of England, he walked around the room moving his hands like the Viceroy and acting like the Viceroy. He was doing what Dustin Hoffman does: becoming the other person so that he could get the other person's point of view. He became Nehru, and then Ali, who was the head of the Muslim Congress. Then Gandhi said, "I'll step back and look at this situation from the eyes of the world."

Part of his negotiation strategy was to take clean, clear perceptual positions and rehearse the other person's point of view so that he could make a much wider range of wise decisions. Coming to a negotiation from only one perspective is limiting; coming from a wide variety of perspectives is very powerful.

Jonas Salk, who discovered the vaccine for polio, is reported to have said, "What would I do as a virus? If I were these virus cells, what would I do?" He "became" the virus, and that perspective gave him new insight.

Einstein didn't come up with the theory of relativity by wearing a white smock and writing a million formulas on a blackboard. He said to himself, "What would it be like to be on the end of a light beam, shooting ahead in space? What if I were on the end of a light beam and I held a mirror in front of me—would I be able to see my face, or would the light not yet be there?" He came up with original ideas by taking different perceptual positions.

What does it do?

- Provides access to resources from the client's life experiences.
- Uses metaphor to discover creative solutions to challenges.

☞ Exercise I

1. Take a moment and remember an argument or a situation where you were intimidated, or a situation where someone did some behavior that resulted in hurt feelings on your part. Choose a situation that is mild to moderately unpleasant.

2. Remember the situation by stepping back into it—see, hear, and feel what occurred from your own point of view (Self). Identify your feelings and your understanding of the experience.

3. Float up and out to a neutral position (watching from above or from the side). Watch yourself and the other person in detail (Observer). Notice how the other person sounds, looks, moves, breathes, and so on. Consider any information you have about her values, personal history, and experience immediately prior to the event you're remembering.

4. Float down into the other person, becoming her as fully as possible, adapting her physiology, perspective, history, and so on. Replay the situation in your mind (fully and completely) from her point of view (Other).

5. Float up and off to the side. Watch the interaction again, with the information from Self and Other. Watch both players.

6. Return to Self. Review the situation again completely.

Answer the following questions:

-   What has changed for you in relation to this memory?
-   Which was easiest to do?
-   How might this be valuable in your life? Your work?

This can be a very useful process to guide a client through when he is confused or upset about another person's or group's behavior.

With partners, appoint three roles: A , B, and C.

A tells a story. B listens for two minutes in each perceptual position (without interacting with A): Self, Observer, and Other. C observes physiological and voice matching. All parties notice the effect of B's shifts in perceptual positions on A. The group shares perceptions of the implications of each position on the communication.

Case Study

Max had an ongoing problem with a co-worker. During a coach session, he revealed that he had just had a run-in with this person and said that the co-worker was "defensive" when he gave her some necessary feedback.

His coach had him relive the experience from the Self position. Max reiterated how angry he felt when he was being "attacked" by this person. His coach had him step back to the Observer position and watch the experience. Here, Max could detach and gather information without getting caught up in his feelings. He then imagined actually being the coworker, standing the way that she did, doing his honest best to take on her viewpoint and life experiences as far as he knew them. He experienced the event through her eyes. When he returned to the Self position, after having "stepped into her" as literally as he could, he realized that his style was intimidating to her. He thought through how he could present information more effectively with her in the future, in a way that would not intimidate her. He later said that he felt empowered by this because he developed a strategy to communicate effectively with her. He never became a victim and avoided playing a blame game.

OPEN QUESTIONS

Why use them?

A primary skill of effective coaching is asking good questions. Use open questions to help the client solve her issue, dig deeper for creative responses, and stimulate articulation of her thinking. This skill is especially useful for the manager-coach to draw out the employee's thinking, to build problem-solving skills, and encourage creativity.

What are they?

These are questions that cannot be easily answered by a simple "yes," "no," or another single word or number. They invite the person to talk further, and they direct the client's attention to a specific aspect of what has been said. Open questions can ask for sensory-specific information. For example, in response to an employee's claim that "My friend is always putting me down!" an open question might be, "How, specifically, does your friend put you down?" or "When, specifically, does she do that?"

How do I do it?

Open questions can ask for more information about the person's desired outcome. "How would you know if this problem was solved?" or "What needs to be different for you to feel good about this?"

Open questions that start with "how" elicit better information that those which start with "why." "Why" questions tend to create defensive responses and elicit excuses, justifications, and explanations. The following exercise will help get you to think about how to structure your questions effectively.

1. A client has been discussing his frustration about the way his previous coach worked with him, which included offering lots of advice.

    ■ Ineffective closed question: "Was there something that you could appreciate about that coach?"

    ■ Possible open question: "Having had that experience, what do you want in a coaching relationship now?"

    ■ Write another useful open question.

2. A client has been telling you that she finds her work a challenge because the company won't provide training.

    ■ Ineffective closed question: "Are you upset about that?"

    ■ Possible open question: "What are the skills that you feel that you need to improve upon?"

    ■ Write another useful open question.

3. A colleague is discussing his feelings of resentment about one of the other workers in his workplace.

    ■ Ineffective closed question: "Have you told him about this?"

    ■ Possible open question: "What do you think might be the best solution for you in dealing with this person?"

    ■ Write another useful open question.

4. A client has just explained that she hated sports as a teenager.

    ■ Ineffective closed question: "Do you hate sports now?"

    ■ Possible open question: "How do you think that affects you now?"

    ■ Write another useful open question.

5.   An unemployed friend tells you he is trying to get a job at a place where you have a contact.

- Ineffective closed question: "Do you want me to ask the boss about it?"
- Possible open question: "How can I help you with that?"
- Write another useful open question.

6.   A client explains that she didn't get the promotion she wanted so she's applied for a job at another company.

- Ineffective closed question: "Do you want to work for them?"
- Possible open question: "Why do you think that they didn't promote you and what might you do next time you apply for a promotion that you want?"
- Write another useful open question.

7.   A client begins to cry about a situation that has arisen.

- Ineffective closed question: "Are you okay?"
- Possible open question: (After acknowledging that it is OK to have these feelings) "Now that you are letting your feelings out, how do you want to deal with this?"
- Write another useful open question.

8.   A client discusses his feelings of depression after he loses his job.

- Ineffective closed question: "If you could be the way you wanted, would you let go of those sad feelings?"
- Possible open question: "You've lost your job, and that's tough. What is your next move?"
- Write another useful open question.

THE META-MODEL

Business is primarily the accomplishment of specific tasks through cooperative effort. The Meta-Model is an excellent tool for business communication because it works to specify communication when it is necessary and appropriate. It provides a method for dealing with what is missing, distorted, or over-generalized in thinking and communicating. The Meta-Model offers some very powerful questions for coaching, and provides a framework for knowing when to ask the right question.

What is it?

The Meta-Model is a set of common language patterns including deletions, distortions, and generalizations.

Many of the NLP techniques used in coaching originated with the Meta-Model. John Grinder and Richard Bandler originally developed the Meta-Model to identify and clarify classes of language patterns in order to improve communication. Bandler and Grinder began this process by modeling change experts Virginia Satir (the originator of family therapy), Milton Erickson (a famous psychiatrist), and Fritz Perls (the developer of Gestalt therapy), who all used Meta-Model inquiries intuitively yet with great skill.

One of the basic presuppositions of NLP is expressed in the metaphor that "the map is not the territory." Maps are useful because they have a similarity to the terrain they depict, but any map will be a limited and incomplete representation of the terrain. The external world, what may be called "reality," is like the terrain. At any given moment, we are bombarded with billions of bits of information. But we can only process a small portion of what we receive from the world. Without our brain's ability to filter information by deleting, distorting, and generalizing input, we would be overwhelmed.

We unconsciously create mental models or maps that serve this filtering function. Our maps select what to attend to, what is important, what events mean, how the world works, etc. We then use these "maps" of the world to guide our behavior and negotiate life.

As a good communicator, it is useful to understand another's "map of the world," and the Meta-Model provides techniques for gathering this information. Our "maps" either empower us or limit us, so our goal is to increase the chances that language will empower us.

What does it do?

- Helps to clarify the thoughts of the speaker for better understanding

- Uses language to draw out a person's model of the world, which is below the surface of thinking

- Helps create change in a person's experience to expand her model of the world, creating more options for thinking, deciding, and understanding

Every word is an anchor for a deeper and often richer set of meanings. For each listener, the same set of words will create different images, that are dependent upon his experience. So if I say, "She showed me something," what literal representations do you have in your mind? Who is she? What is she showing me? How is she showing it to me? You might ask, "Who is showing you what and how are they showing you?" I could then respond, "My dog Penny showed me her puppy by carrying it to me in her mouth."

The Meta-Model distinctions fall into three identifying sets:

1. GATHERING INFORMATION (DELETIONS)

- Noun Deletions (who, what, which, where, or when is left out)

- Comparative Deletions (there is an implied comparison)

- Lack of Referential Index (unspecified person, place, or thing

- Unspecified Processes (the "how" of it is unclear—the process is vague)

- Nominalizations (an active process is mentally changed into a static thing)

2. LIMITS OF THE SPEAKER'S MODEL (GENERALIZATIONS)

- Universal Quantifiers: Absolutes (all, always, never, nobody, and so on)

- Modal Operators of Necessity (should, must, have to, and so on)

- Modal Operators of Impossibility (can't, impossible, not able to, and so on)

- Lost Performatives (overgeneralized judgments)

3. SEMANTIC ILL-FORMEDNESS

- Cause and Effect (a claim that something outside a person is causing her to have an emotional response)

- Mind Reading (a claim that one knows what another is thinking or feeling)

- Presuppositions (assumptions that are implied in the speaker's language)

To learn to use the Meta-Model, you need to be able to hear the distinctions and respond with an appropriate Meta-Model question.

SIMPLE DELETION

With simple deletions, the subject and /or object of the sentence is missing or unclear. To recover it, ask, "Who or what, specifically?"

- Sample: "I'm happy"
- Meta-Model Response: "About what, specifically?"

UNSPECIFIED "WHO" (REFERENTIAL INDEX)

In this instance, words and phrases in the speaker's language do not identify who is being referred to. If the word or phrase fails to identify a specific person or thing, the listener has identified a generalization.

- Sample: "People are a problem."
- Meta-Model inquiry: "Who, specifically?" or "What, specifically?" or
  "Which _____, specifically?"
- Sample: "They said to contact you."
- Meta-Model Response: "Who, specifically, said to contact me?"

COMPARATIVE DELETIONS

Comparative deletions occur when an implied comparison is being made in the speaker's mind, but it is not clear what is being compared to what. Some of the key words to listen for include "enough," "too," "better," "best," and "most." The Meta-Model response is "As compared to what (or whom)?"

META-MODEL

Learn the Meta–Model Distinctions

The Meta–Model is a set of linguistic distinctions that allows you to understand a speaker's experience and get more precise information about the person's "map or model" of the world.

The Distinctions Fall Into 3 Sets

Gather information

Recognizing limits of the speaker's map or model

Recognizing semantic gaps

Listen For Cues

These are linguistic cues for each distinction of which the attentive listener will be aware.

Ask Appropriate Meta–Model Questions

For each linguistic cue, there is a specific question that allows you to gather information, challenge limitations, or fill in the gaps in the speaker's presentation.

Maintain Rapport

Meta–Model questions probe into another person's world. Be sure to maintain rapport and use good judgement about the use of these tools!

- Sample: "This computer is too expensive."
- Meta-Model Response: "It's too expensive compared to what?"

NOMINALIZATIONS

Nominalizations occur when an active process is changed into a static thing. The purpose of recognizing nominalizations is to assist the speaker in reconnecting his linguistic model with the ongoing processes in his experience.

When nominalizations are used, static images are created in the mind of the listener and speaker. The use of the Meta-Model in this case turns the static images into moving pictures, which provides a lot more information at the conscious level.

You can turn a static image into a mental movie by changing the nominalized word to an active word using an "-ing" form. For example, change "relationship" to "relating," "information" to "informing," and so on. When something can't easily be turned into an "-ing" word, you can ask, "How, specifically?"

- Sample: "Mary is awfully passive for a being such a free spirited person."
- Meta-Model Response: "How exactly is Mary passive?" "What do you mean by 'free spirited?'"
- Sample: "My confusion prevents me from moving ahead."
- Meta-Model Response: "What is confusing you, and how?"

UNSPECIFIED VERBS

Unspecified verbs are those that lack the specificity needed to completely understand the meaning intended in the communication. (All verbs can be further specified.) The Meta-Model inquiry is "How, specifically?"

- Sample: "My father scares me."
- Meta-Model Response: "Scares you how?"

UNIVERSAL QUANTIFIERS

Universal quantifiers are absolutes in the linguistic world. These are phrases such as "never," "all," "every," "always," and "no one." They are words that over generalize from a few experiences to a whole class of experience. One way to use the Meta-Model with absolutes is to backtrack the absolute word but exaggerate it with your tone of voice: "ALL? Really?" Another way is to chunk down the generalization by asking, "Who (or what) specifically?"

☞ **Examples:**

- "She never arrives anywhere on time!"
- Meta-Model Response: "NEVER?" "It is your experience that she is never on time? For anything!?"
- "It is impossible to get anything done on time."
- Meta-Model Response: "Has there ever been a time when you did get something done on time?"

☞ **The procedure can be outlined as follows:**

Step 1. Listen to the speaker's language, identifying universal quantifiers.

Step 2. Inquire about the universality of the generalization.

- Sample: "You work all the time!"
- Meta-Model Response: "I work ALL the time? Is that truly your experience?"

MODAL OPERATORS OF NECESSITY

Modal operators of necessity are statements identifying rules about or limits to a person's behavior. Examples of modal operators related to necessity are "should/shouldn't," "must/must not," and "have to." To inquire about these limits, ask, "What stops you?" or "What would happen if you did (didn't)?"

Asking, "What stops you?" helps the person think about what experience(s) she had where she created this generalization. Asking, "What would happen if you did (didn't)?" gets the speaker to consider consequences. Avoid asking "Why?" It sometimes might work to unearth high-quality information but more often will get defensiveness, explanations, or justifications.

☞ Samples:

- "I have to get everything done."
- Meta-Model Response: "What stops you?"
- "I shouldn't tell them how I feel about that."
- Meta-Model Response: "What would happen if you did?"

☞ Sample:

- "Our new project must be completed by year's end!"
- Meta-Model Response: "Please tell me, what would happen if it isn't completed?"

MODAL OPERATORS OF IMPOSSIBILITY

Modal operators of impossibility are statements that describe what is considered impossible in the speaker's map of the world. They are identified by words such as "can't," "impossible," "not possible," and so on. Many people limit their world unnecessarily by thinking something difficult or unfamiliar is "impossible." It is often useful to challenge this limited thinking by asking, "What would happen if you could?"

Notice how these questions are typically more useful than asking, "Why?" which often leads to rationalizations, defensiveness or explanations.

- "I can't apply for the promotion."
- Meta-Model Response: "What is stopping you from applying?"

LOST PERFORMATIVES

Lost performatives (where the performer is not identified) are judgments that a person makes that he believes to be true about the world. These are generalizations based on his own map of the world. They are identified by words such as "best," "good," "bad," "stupid," "annoying," "right," "wrong," "true," "false," and so on. To inquire about a Lost performative, ask: "For whom?" or "According to whom?" or even (gently) "Who says?" You can also ask for evidence: "How do you know?"

The mental strategy for using the Meta-Model inquiry with Lost performatives can be described as follows:

Step 1: Listen to the speaker's language for generalizations about the world—these are identified with words in the same class as stupid, annoying, right, wrong, true, false, and so on.

Step 2: Identify that this is a generalization about the speaker's model of the world.

Step 3: Since this is a generalization about the model and not about the world, the coach may help the speaker to develop more possibilities within his model.

- "It's bad to be late."

- Meta-Model Response: "Bad for whom?"

- "This is the right way to behave."

- Meta-Model Response: "This is the right way for whom to do it?"

CAUSE AND EFFECT

A Cause-and-Effect Meta-Model violation is made when a person claims that someone or a situation or thing is creating an internal response in her that does not exist in reality, or where the connection is not clear. The Meta-Model inquiry is, "How does X cause Y?"

☞ Samples:

- "This music annoys me."

- Meta-Model Response: "How exactly does this music cause you to be annoyed?"

- Over-generalize: "He makes me mad."

- Meta-Model Response: "How does his behavior make you mad?"

MIND READING

Mind reading happens when a person claims to know what another individual is thinking or what is motivating the other person without any specific communication from the speaker about what is in his mind.

The Meta-Model inquiry for this pattern is, "How do you know X?" This provides a way for the speaker to become aware of and even to question those assumptions that she may have taken for granted.

- "My dad doesn't care what I do."

- Meta-Model Response: "How do you know that your dad doesn't care?"

- "You're not going to like this, but ..."

- Meta-Model Response: "How do you know that?"

- "I know you will think that this is a stupid question, but ..."

- Meta-Model Response: "How do you know I'll think that it is stupid?"

PRESUPPOSITIONS (SILENT OR HIDDEN ASSUMPTIONS)

Presuppositions are (sometimes unconscious) assumptions that a person makes. In identifying presuppositions, the goal is to help the speaker identify those basic assumptions that narrow her model of the world and limit behavioral possibilities. Linguistically, these basic assumptions show up as presuppositions of the person's language. For example, to make sense out of the sentence, "I'm afraid that the new manager is as untrustworthy as the last one," you have to accept as true the idea that the original manager was untrustworthy.

To identify presuppositions, ask yourself, "What must be true or assumed for the person saying this?"

The Meta-Model response unmasks the silent assumption by asking for evidence or by backtracking the hidden assumption. Consider this statement: "If my boss knew how overburdened I am, he wouldn't keep dumping more responsibility on me." This sentence assumes that the person is overburdened, that her boss is unaware of how overburdened she is, and that her boss's behavior would change if he knew about her feelings.

Possible questions include the following: "How do you get yourself overburdened?" or "How do you know that your boss is unaware of this?" or "How do you know that he is dumping on you rather than entrusting you with responsibility?"

Sample

- "Since Monty is so mean, let's avoid him." What within the sentence must be true? Monty is mean; he should be avoided.

- Meta-Model Response: "How is Monty mean?" "What will avoiding him get for us?"

CRAFT OF COACHING

The coaching "crafts" below are a set of specific skills that can be used in coaching sessions. These are the "nuts and bolts" of coaching and are especially useful for coaching employees. The manager-coach can easily incorporate many of these patterns in his communication, although it is best to "switch hats" into the coaching role when using them.

ACKNOWLEDGING

What is it?

Acknowledging the client is acknowledging her deeper self. For example, the coach might say, "I know that you must be disappointed about not receiving the promotion—you definitely worked hard and were well-prepared for it." It is "seeing" the client.

Why use it?

Often what's really going on with a person is not acknowledged, but when the coach articulates it, it becomes part of the conversation. It is different from praising. Praising is making a judgment or an evaluation of a person; acknowledging is about stating what is.

What does it do?

It creates a deeper rapport with the client.

☞ Exercise

Identify five people that you know. Write an acknowledgment of who they are or who they have been to get to where they are today. In addition, how might you acknowledge yourself for who you are or what you have done to become the person that you are now? Take a few moments, and make a list of your accomplishments.

CHALLENGING

What is it?

Challenging is suggesting that your client do something that would take him well beyond his comfort zone. It must be a strong enough challenge that your client will actually resist it. For example, if you have a workaholic client whose life is out of balance, you might challenge him to take two hours a day for pure personal fun and recreation. He may say that there's no way that can happen and give you a lot of reasons. You now have a place to begin negotiating for something that will move him toward what he really wants. If he is in conflict, this step will typically identify both sides of the issue, which you can then help him resolve.

Why use it?

Challenging is helpful in two ways. The first is that it gets your client to stretch beyond where she would go on her own. There is truth to the saying "Life winners stretch themselves ten percent beyond their comfort zone."

The second way challenge is helpful is that it demonstrates you believe in your client and that she has what it takes to move beyond where she thought she could go.

What does it do?

It motivates the client to go beyond where he would normally go on his own.

☞ Exercise

Work with two friends. Each should identify three areas of their personal or work life that are out of balance, and write them down. In the group describe these imbalances. Your partners then work together to devise a challenge to each area that takes you beyond your comfort zone. Negotiate a counter-offer with them.

INTRUDING

What is it?

Intruding is a way of politely interrupting your client so that she doesn't go on and on in some way that is not useful during the coach session. While coaching, you might intrude by doing the following:

1. Backtrack your understanding of the story so far. In other words, you give the summary. Limit your summary to a few well-backtracked sentences. Backtracking means you feed back what you hear to the speaker. For example, the speaker says, " I really want to move ahead on this project, it is very important to me." You interrupt and say, " So it is very important to you..."

2. Tell him that you are going to interrupt him. "I need to interrupt you for a moment" or "Excuse me, I'm not certain where we are going with this."

3. Use Meta-Model questions, such as "How specifically?" or "Where specifically?" or "Tell me what you mean by that."

4. Redirect the conversation toward a more useful topic by asking something like, "What did you learn from that?" or "What did having this experience mean to you?"

5. Identify a positive intention for the long story: "I know you're going somewhere important with this story; what is it that you are really wanting now?"

Intruding is a useful skill for making the best use of coach time.

☞ Exercise

The client is telling a long rambling story, something she can go on and on about. As the client is telling the story, a coach's job is to interrupt her and help to change the course of the story by trying out different coach skills. Ask her to summarize: "What does that mean to you?"

INQUIRY

What is it?

Milton Erickson, considered one of the world's foremost hypnotherapists and one of the early models for NLP, kept a number of objects in his office: small ornaments, unusual pencils, little figurines, and so on. At the end of a therapeutic session, Milton would often hand his client an object, telling the client that there is something with deep meaning for him in the object and that he should concentrate on it between their sessions. The client would often find that something important bubbled up from his unconscious mind through this experience. As a coaching skill, inquiry taps into this idea.

Why use it?

This is a powerful way for the client to maintain a conscious focus of attention on a new way of being in the world.

What does it do?

Inquiry is asking questions for reflection and self-discovery. With your inquiry, you offer a question to a client for her to ponder until you meet again. It is not necessarily a question that has a "right" answer.

Inquiry questions could include the following:

- "What is my state of mind when I'm doing my best?"
- "What am I postponing?"
- "What am I holding back?"
- "What do I say 'yes' to, and what do I say 'no' to?"
- "What am I settling for?"
- "What do I really want here and now?"

The book *Coactive Coaching* has a long list of inquiry questions. Some coaches maintain lists of inquiry questions from which they can choose.

☞ Exercise

In a small group, brainstorm several useful inquiry questions for the following coach contexts: motivation, follow-through, identifying what's working in your life, and getting past stuck places.

REQUESTING

What is it?

You can make a request of your client. Of course, you will only request what is relevant to your client's agenda. You might, for example, request that your client take action on something that he's been procrastinating about. You might also turn a client's complaint into an opportunity by suggesting that he consider making a request of someone else.

Why use it?

Requesting is used to nudge the client forward. For example, if your client complains that her boss does not read her reports in a timely way, you might suggest that she make a request of the boss. Notice how this re-empowers the client and keeps her from getting stuck in "victim mode."

How do I do it?

When you request that the client complete some assignment, follow through on something, or try out something new, it is important to remain unattached to your idea. Even if you're pretty clear that your idea would be very helpful to the client, it is up to him to answer in one of three ways: he can say yes, he can say no, or he can come up with a different possibility. If he says yes, employ the coaching craft of accountability. If he says no, you can ask him what he will do or how he wants to approach dealing with his issue. If he makes a counter-offer, you can again employ accountability: "Would you like to be held accountable for this?"

☞ Exercise

With a friend, list five areas of life in which you have a complaint. Your partner should devise a request that addresses each complaint. To each request, you can say yes or no or make a counter-offer.

CONTENT REFRAMING

What is it?

Reframing is putting something into a different framework or context than it has been previously perceived. It helps to expand the client's possibilities. For example, imagine that a friend of yours walks by in the morning and does not respond to your friendly "hello." There are many meanings you could take from this, and they will depend on your experience, your beliefs, and your mood. You might think that she simply didn't hear you, or that she doesn't like you, or that she's angry, or that she's rude for some reason, and so on.

Why use it?

Most clients spend much of their time thinking within the mental boxes that they have constructed in their lives. When clients display limited thinking, reframing offers new possibilities for understanding a situation in a broader way.

You can use the following exercise to reframe a problem and bring a new perspective to it.

Think of something that is annoying, that causes you concern (your child got a "D" on a test, your boss seems grumpy, and so on). Then ask your client (or yourself):

- How important will this be in ten years?
- In relation to all of the things the person does and all of their actions, behaviors, and traits, how important is this?
- How does this actually impact my life?
- Name five things that this situation could mean that would not cause you the same concern.
- Reverse the limiting presuppositions. Ask: "How is the opposite of what you thought actually true?"

ONE-PHRASE REFRAMING

Inspired by Robert Dilts, One-Phrase Reframing reframes pejorative statements about oneself or about others. The purpose is to help clients move past self-sabotaging limits by rephrasing the key words or statements that they make when describing their limitations.

For example: Notice how the words in these groups get progressively less pejorative, but could mean the same thing:

- cheap – frugal – thrifty
- compromising – considerate– respectful
- stuck in his head – mental – intelligent – brilliant
- selfish – aware of his own needs – looks after himself

Applying One–Phrase Reframes

Change a word that has a limiting or negative connotation to a new word or phrase that is more positive or gives a wider perspective. Have the client finish the statement: "I stop myself because I _____." The client may say something like the following:

- "I stop myself because I don't want to be criticized by someone."
- "I stop myself because I am afraid I'll fail."
- "I stop myself because I'll look foolish."
- "I stop myself because I feel awkward about meeting new people."

Reframe using a new word with a more positive meaning or a wider context (time, people, or space). For example, you can change "look foolish" to "take a risk."

- Client: "I stop myself because I am afraid I'll fail."

  - *Possible coach reframe:* "I'm confident that you have all the resources you need to meet this challenge (or take this risk)."

- Client: "I stop myself because I am afraid I'll look foolish."

  - *Possible coach reframe:* "It can be helpful to be sensitive about how you come across to others."

- Client: "I stop myself because I am afraid I'll get criticized."

  - *Possible coach reframe:* "I'll bet you can find the usefulness in any feedback."

- Client: "I stop myself because I am afraid I feel awkward meeting new people."

  - *Possible coach reframe:* "It's good to be clear about your present state so that you can move beyond it."

Managing Client Sessions

COACH SESSION OVERVIEW

Each coaching session is a process in itself and the coach can use the "Coach Session Overview" to manage the steps within a coaching session. It covers everything from the pre-session preparation to post-session notes and follow-up. The coach can use this map to keep on track with the client in each session.

GAINING RAPPORT

Rapport can be defined as being "in sync" or "on the same wavelength" or "in harmony" with another person. It implies clear understanding and mutual credibility between two or more people.

The ingredients in rapport were an early discovery from modeling through NLP. Mirroring or matching certain aspects of a client's behavior creates natural rapport. These include her posture, her breathing, the tone and tempo and volume of her speech, and the process words she uses. When rapport is achieved, the mirroring becomes mutual.

Why use it?

When natural rapport occurs, the speaker and listener are "in sync," the communication flows smoothly, and both parties easily understand each other. A deep level of rapport is a requirement for effective coaching.

THE COACHING SESSION

1
Pre-Session

- Preparing for the session
- Make space for the client
- Set intention for the session
- Prepare your state (curiosity, not knowing, respect for the client, NLP Presuppositions)

2
Rapport

- Creating Trust
- Ease with the client
- Noticing when rapport is breaking down and correcting

3
Directionalizing

- Open questions that you tailor for the person
- Consequences of different openings

4
Holding Space

- Maintaining the focus
- Listening and backtracking
- Getting specific
- Listening beyond content—attending to process

5
What's called for?

- Coach flexibility
- Fostering flexibility in the client

6
Planning/Action

- Movement
- Decisions
- Identifiable steps
- Evaluation of the plan

7
Closure/Follow-up

- Backtrack of the session
- Review Accountability/Inquiry/assignment
- Bridge to next meeting (date and time)
- After session notes–issues, metaphors, "short hand"

What does it do?

Bandler and Grinder, developers of NLP, modeled these processes from exquisite communicators such as Milton Erickson and Virginia Satir. These communicators were able to create deep empathy with the people with whom they connected and were able to lead the conversation as well. Practicing these methods will allow you to create rapport quickly even with clients with whom you find it hard to connect.

How do I do it?

Rapport is gained by matching the thinking process of the other person. People think in three primary modes: Visual (picturing in the mind's eye), kinesthetic (feelings, internal sensations) and auditory (words and tones, talking to one's self).

We all think by picturing things, talking to ourselves, and having feelings. One mode, however, tends to be dominant and more in conscious awareness. When someone communicates with us using our favored mode, we will understand her better and relate to what she is communicating more easily. Developing the ability to match another's communication gives us flexibility in our communications and generally results in heightened rapport.

How can you determine a person's lead mode?

Notice his posture, how he holds his feet, the angle of his head, and where he has his hands. Mirror this posture. Convincer: Try having a conversation where you first mismatch the other person's posture, then match it. Notice the difference.

Match the rhythm and speed of another person's breathing. Convincer: Try having a conversation where you first mismatch the other person's breathing, then match it. Notice the difference.

Match the tempo and tonality of the other person's speech. Convincer: Try having a conversation where you first mismatch the other person's voice, then match it. Notice the difference.

Match the process words used (predicates that identify which of the sensory modes a person is thinking in: visual, auditory, or kinesthetic). Through the process words, or "predicates," people consistently report how they are thinking. It takes a little listening practice to identify these words, but it is definitely worth the effort:

Common Visual Predicates:

- See ("I see what you mean.")
- Picture ("I can't picture that.")
- Perspective ("Get a new perspective.")
- Blank ("I just went blank.")
- Look ("Look at this!")
- Image ("I need a clearer image of the problem.")
- Colorful ("A colorful example is …")

Common Auditory Predicates:

- Rings a bell ("This rings a bell!")
- Static ("She gives me a lot of static.")
- Tone ("I don't like the tone of this.")
- Say ("I'm only going to say this once.")
- Listen ("Listen …")
- Clicked ("Things just clicked for me.")
- Tells ("Something tells me I should …")

Common Kinesthetic Predicates:

- Feel ("I really feel good about this.")
- Touch ("Get in touch with me.")
- Cold ("He's cold and insensitive.")
- Walk ("Walk me through this problem.")
- Get a handle ("I can't get a handle on this.")
- Reach ("I keep reaching for a decision.")
- Solid ("Let's get a solid understanding of this.")

WATCH NON-VERBAL BEHAVIOR

Visual

When you are thinking in pictures, you tend to breathe higher in the chest and more shallowly. You'll tend to talk rapidly and in high voice tones. Your shoulders are held upright and straight across.

Kinesthetic

When you are into your feelings, you tend to breathe more deeply, low in the stomach area. You talk more slowly and in deeper tones, and you pause longer between words and sentences. Your shoulders will be more sloped and more relaxed.

Auditory

There are two types of auditory thinking: tonal and words. When you are more aware of tonality, you'll speak in a tempo somewhere between the visual or kinesthetic thinkers, with a rich or musical tonality. You'll breathe evenly in the diaphragm or with the whole chest, often with a prolonged exhale. Your posture may be the "saxophone position" (how you'd look if you were playing the saxophone, with the shoulders pushed back). When you are thinking in words or listening to your internal dialogue, you might touch your hand to your chin, cock your head to one side, or breathe shallowly.

HOLDING THE CLIENT'S AGENDA

In today's world, it is difficult to stay focused on our goals because we are faced with a thousand distractions on a daily basis. Coaching helps us stay on track. Holding the client's agenda is a primary job of a coach.

Purpose:

- To help the client keep focused.
- To provide boundaries for the client.

Method

- Work with the client to establish an agreed agenda. This may include two levels:
  - The larger set of values, dreams, and goals for which the client wishes to use coaching. These are usually identified in the intake session or re-contracting sessions.
  - The specific agenda established for the session.
- There are many methods for holding the client's agenda:
  - Stating the agenda and restating it at specific times.
  - Backtracking and relating topics to agenda items.
  - Asking powerful questions based on the client's agenda.
  - Intruding when the client goes off agenda.
  - Challenging relevancy when the client goes off agenda.
  - Pointing out conflicts in agenda items.

DIRECTIONALIZING THE COMMUNICATION

What is it?

Using your words and language structure to direct the conversation in a purposeful way. This is a skill that can make a tremendous difference in the outcome of a coach session or meeting. The first few words that the coach utters will set a direction. If the coach asks, "How has it been going since our last coach conversation?" He will probably get a vague answer, or will get a lot of information that may not be useful for the coach session. If he says, "What is our goal for today?" He will usually get a specific direction that the client wants to head into that is much more useful.

Why use it?

When you "directionalize," you use language to lead a person or group's experience and increase the likelihood of the experience being successful. As is mentioned above, doing so helps to avoid getting too much content or irrelevant content for the coaching session. With this coaching skill, you direct the coach conversation in a useful way. You can use certain patterns that assume a direction. These are statements, words, or phrases that create an assumption in a sentence, and they include some very powerful language patterns of influence.

There are several types of key presuppositions:

- Time. This category presupposes that something will occur, and it is just a matter of when. Some of the time presuppositions are "when," "before," "since," "after," "next week," and so on.

  - The sentence "Do you want to sign the contract before we have lunch?" presupposes that the contract will be signed.

- The sentence "Since we are meeting today, we can finish off the X project" presupposes that we are meeting and that we can finish the project.

- Or/ordinal. These presuppositions provide for a choice between options. Ordinal presuppositions put something into a sequence:

  - The sentence "Shall we meet at your office or mine?" presupposes that we are going to meet; it is only a matter of where.

  - The sentence "Will this be the first time that you have identified your personal criteria for work that motivates you?" presupposes that you will set your criteria.

- Adverbs and adjectives. These words modify sentences and add a descriptor. Notice that any "ly" word can be used as a presupposition.

  - "I'm wondering how quickly you can identify the goals for your project." This sentence assumes that you will set your goals, and the only question is the speed of your completion.

  - "Fortunately, the whole team will be present, so all the questions can be answered." The assumption is that questions will be answered.

- Awareness. These presuppositions assume that something is the case and the only question is whether or not you are aware of it. Awareness presuppositions include "aware," "realize," "recognize," "know," "see," "caught on," and so on.

  - "Are you aware of how often you already use these forms of language?" This sentence assumes that you use presuppositions, and it directs your attention to whether or not you are aware of this fact.

- "It won't take our clients long to figure out that we provide the most timely service." This sentence presupposes that we provide the "most timely" service. The listener's attention is directed to the client's realizing the fact.

With two friends create a group of three: A, B, and C. Write out a typical opening statement of three or four sentences that you might make as a coach when opening a coach session, after you've said your amenities. With assistance from A and B, identify the following:

- What is presupposed?

- What is the internal response of the listener? What is assumed in his internal experience as a result of the statement?

- Revise your "directionalizing" statement to direct the listener in the way that you want.

A trainer opens a new-employee orientation session with the statement, "I hope that this session is not too elementary for you." What is presupposed in the statement? Where does it direct the listener's attention? How might the trainer restate it so that it moves the session along in a positive way? Notice the difference when the trainer says, "By the end of this session, you will know five things that are essential for your success here."

A manager opens a meeting by saying, "I know that everyone's mind is on the X project, but before talking about that, there are a couple of things I want to get out of the way." The whole group mentally checked out until he got back to project X. He later said that he was trying to acknowledge the team's main concern, but he did need to cover all the topics. It might have been better to say something like, "I know that everyone's mind is on project X, but before we discuss that, there are two critical informational items that you need to know about."

Important coach implications: A coach opens a coach session by saying, "Tell me how it's been going since our last session." Put yourself in the client's position. What is your internal process? You are required to sort through a lot of information and try to pick out the relevant pieces. It is a very vague request. Useful possibilities for opening a coaching session include the following statements:

- "What is our agenda for today?"

- "Where are you now, and where do you want to be by the end of this session?"

- "What do you want to accomplish today?"

- "Before we discuss your goals for today, tell me how it went for you on last week's plan."

Each of these opening statements will direct the coach conversation in a useful way. Always remember to get clear about your goal before you get started. Once you know your goal, it is easy to lead the conversation in a productive way.

OUTCOMES

REQUIREMENTS FOR SUCCESS

People are more committed to goals they set for themselves and that arise out of their desires and interests than to goals others give them. The process of creating well-formed outcomes comes directly from NLP and is especially useful for the manager-coach because it provides specific questions that can help an employee formulate powerful goals.

What is it?

This set of 12 questions represents the requirements for ensuring a well-formed outcome – in other words, an outcome that should be ecological and appropriate and that will be achieved if the questions are answered properly.

Why use it?

Most outcomes are not really well-formed, and thus have less potential for success than if they were. By responding to each question, the client has a much better chance of success. When an outcome is clear and not resisted by any inner forces within the individual, the client will organize his/her unconscious processes around it to achieve it.

How do you use it?

Asking the following questions meets the requirements to help ensure success:

1. What do you want?

   - Is the outcome:

     - Stated in the positive? (What you do want, not what you don't want.)
     - Be initiated by you?
     - Is the outcome controlled by you?
     - Of a manageable chunk size? (Break it down into smaller outcomes if necessary.)

2. How will you know when you've got it?

     - What is the evidence? (In sensory based terms: see, hear, feel, smell, taste.)

3. Where, when and with whom do you want it? (Context)

4. What are the positive and negative consequences of getting your outcome?

5. What resources do you need to get your outcome? (Information, attitude, internal state, training, money; help or support from others, etc.)

6. What are you already doing to begin to achieve your outcome?

7. What will achieving that outcome get for you? (Determine the real benefit beyond just getting the specific outcome.)

8. Is the first step to achieving your outcome specific and achievable?

9. Is there more than one way to get your outcome?

10. What time-frames are involved?

11. What stops you from having your outcome now?

12. Imagine stepping into the future and having your outcome fully. Look back and determine what steps were required to achieve the outcome now that you have it. ("Backwards planning")

META-OUTCOME
(OR THE OUTCOME OF THE OUTCOME)

What is it?

Most of the goals we set are really means to a greater end. Meta-outcome goes beyond an initial goal to identify the dream or desire that the initial goal serves.

- To find critical motivational patterns and get beyond poorly formed goals.

- To resolve conflicts between parts of oneself or between people.

- To lead you to the client's real criteria.

- Identifies what really motivates you (or a client) toward a goal.

- Uncovers critical values or criteria.

- Identifies the interest in a negotiation.

- Identifies the benefit behind a feature or an activity.

When addressing meta-outcomes with an individual:

Start with a goal or outcome. This can be any goal, but it is especially useful when a goal does not meet the criteria for a "well-formed outcome." An example of a poorly formed outcome would be, "I want the customers to show me more respect."

Imagine the outcome is actually fulfilled and ask, "What would having this outcome fulfilled (customers treat you with respect) do for you?" You are asking for the outcome of the outcome. The client might say, "If customers treat me with more respect, I will feel confident handling their complaints."

Notice whether or not the answer is stated positively and is truly within the person's control. Does the answer include an inner state or a value? "Confidence" is an inner state.

If the answer is not stated positively or is outside the person's control, then repeat the meta-outcome question with the goal from the answer. For instance, the response, "The customers wouldn't be so abusive," is stated negatively and is outside of the person's control. You would repeat the meta-outcome question with the following question: "If the customers weren't so abusive, what would that do for you?" If the response is, "It would be easier to do my job," this is stated positively and may be within the person's control. It would be worthwhile to ask the meta-outcome question again to get to an inner state or value: "And if your job was truly easier as a consequence, what would that do for you?" "Then I would feel more confidence."

Repeat back the key words and phrases and confirm them with the client. "So, what you really want is to feel more confidence when dealing with your customers. Is that right?"

Using meta-outcome to resolve conflict between people: Listen to the position advocated by each party and backtrack the positions to ensure understanding.

Ask each party what fulfillment of their position would do for them. The idea is to move beyond conflicting positions to higher-level motivation. Continue asking the meta-outcome question until you arrive at a shared outcome or at outcomes that are compatible.

Point out to the parties how they both want the same or similar goals, and then use this frame to gain cooperation and resolve the conflict.

☞ Questions to Determine Meta-Outcomes

1. "What will having that get (or do) for you?"

2. "How is that of value to you?"

META-OUTCOME

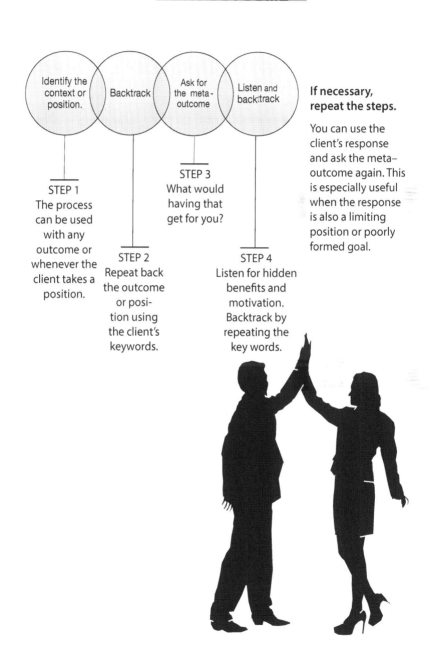

Identify the context or position.

Backtrack

Ask for the meta-outcome

Listen and backtrack

If necessary, repeat the steps.

You can use the client's response and ask the meta-outcome again. This is especially useful when the response is also a limiting position or poorly formed goal.

STEP 1
The process can be used with any outcome or whenever the client takes a position.

STEP 2
Repeat back the outcome or position using the client's keywords.

STEP 3
What would having that get for you?

STEP 4
Listen for hidden benefits and motivation. Backtrack by repeating the key words.

3. "What is your goal in doing that?"

4. "What will that allow you to do, or to have, or to be?"

■ Set the context and state a position (outcome). Examples of positions:

"I am going to starve myself to lose weight."

"I can't apply for that job that I want."

"I need to be responsible for everything that happens in my office."

"I want to be able to stay calm when my wife/husband yells at me."

Backtrack your understanding of the client's position and ask one of the meta-outcome questions.

Case Study

Jack, the manager of a new marketing campaign, had been out of the office for one week on company business. Before leaving, he found out there was some tension between Mike and Sandy, and he was surprised to find it had escalated to the point of threatening the functioning of the whole project team. He knew that he needed to act quickly to resolve the matter.

He brought Mike and Sandy together for a meeting to resolve the conflict. Jack started by taking the time to learn the positions of each party and then to ask each person some meta-outcome questions.

Mike felt that Sandy was taking short-cuts and compromising quality. He wanted her to slow down, attend to the details more, and talk with him before she took certain actions. When asked what having Sandy behave this way would do for him, Mike said that it would ensure that the project was done right. Jack repeated the meta-outcome question, and Mike answered that having the project done right would make the company look good and that he would feel a sense of accomplishment. Going one step further, Mike said that this outcome would mean the project was a success and that he would be proud to have worked on it.

Sandy felt that Mike was holding everything up. She wanted Mike to "loosen up" and be more creative in addressing needs rather than doing everything by the book. Jack asked her what having Mike behave this way would do for her, and she replied that it would free her up to get things done without worrying about Mike's demands. Jack continued with meta-outcome questions, and Sandy reported that being freed up to get things done would mean that they could get the project done successfully and, ideally, ahead of schedule. And this would allow her and the project team to stand out in the company.

As they spoke about their meta-outcomes, Mike and Sandy both realized that they wanted the same general goal: a successful project outcome. They were also surprised to learn that they both wanted to be proud of the project. This point of agreement gave them inspiration to find a working compromise. Sandy agreed to talk with Mike ahead of time on specific matters, and Mike agreed to be open to alternative solutions as long as product quality was not compromised. The tensions that previously threatened the whole project were resolved in a single meeting of less than thirty minutes simply by asking meta-outcome questions!

STORYBOARDING YOUR FUTURE

BACKWARD PLANNING FOR LONG-TERM GOALS

What is it?

Storyboarding is a process of backward planning key steps toward accomplishing your goal and making dreams come true. This is a great tool for coaching employees because it teaches them how to make a road-map to achieving long term goals and maintaining their own motivation.

Why use it?

- To build a bridge between the current state and a long-term goal.

What does it do?

- Provides a link between current activities and long-term goals.

- Identifies major milestones to mark progress toward long-term goals.

How do I do it?

1. Create a well-formed outcome with a rich, full representation of a long-term desirable future. Determine an appropriate time frame for completion of the goal (six months, one year, three years, and so on).

2. Identify the halfway point between now and the desired future. For instance, if the goal were one year away, this "midpoint" would be six months away. Identify what could be happening at the midpoint that would be clear and strong indicators of progress toward the desired goal. Using these indicators, create a representation of this halfway point, and

place it in the appropriate spot between now and the desired future. Do the same for the quarter point.

3. Create a halfway point between now and the quarter point. This will be an "eighth point" on the way to the final goal. For instance, if the goal is one year, the midpoint is six months, the quarter point is three months, and the eighth point is six weeks away. Identify what could be happening at this eighth point that would be clear and strong indicators of progress toward the quarter point and, hence, the goal. Using these indicators, create a representation of this eighth-point milestone and place it in the appropriate spot between now and the quarter point.

4. Identify the next steps that are already under way or that can be taken immediately that move toward the "eighth point" outlined in Step 3.

5. Create a line that goes from the goal-setter (at "Now") through all of the above points and directly to the desired goal in order to create a strong and clear connection between all of these steps. Doing so will make the long-term goal an inevitable consequence of the steps along the way.

6. Test to find out how attainable the goal seems now with a storyboard that links all the appropriate stages to the desired goal.

Case Study

Mark had studied diligently for several years to become a mediator. He wanted to start a mediation practice but felt overwhelmed and did not know where to start. Storyboarding his future seemed an excellent way to proceed. First, he defined the long-term goal by specifying the conditions and details of the outcome. Mark wanted to work four days per week, five hours per day, and provide at least seventy-five hours of direct mediation services per month. He was transitioning out of employment with the state of California and wanted to maintain an income. He also thought that he could use his experience to work with government employees but was not limiting himself to this population. He believed that he could accomplish this goal in eighteen months.

At the halfway point (nine months), he would have an established mediation practice with a minimum of thirty client-contact hours per month, or about eight hours per week. He would have a fully developed Web site, have established a network of referral sources, have written at least two articles for publication

in local papers, and be actively marketing his services. He would be getting referrals from satisfied clients. He would have reduced his state employment to part-time hours or about twenty-four hours per week.

At the quarter-way point of four and a half months (eighteen weeks), he would be providing ten hours of mediation per month. He would have designed and published the Web site. He would have a network of potential referral sources, including attorneys and financial planners. He would have joined the local Chamber of Commerce and at least one other networking source. He would have reduced his work time with the state to thirty-two hours per week.

At the eighth point (nine weeks), he would have started marketing his mediation services and have at least two clients. He would have discussed his long-term plans with his manager at the state, whom he felt was supportive of his goals, and created a plan for reduced time.

Mark was already taking steps by completing his mediation training. He was working on identifying his strengths as a mediator and drafting a write-up of his philosophy of mediation for inclusion on his Web site. These topics became the focus of the immediate coaching activity. Moreover, he began conducting research on how to set up an account for accepting credit cards, and he had gotten support from his wife to begin setting up an office at home.

At the end of the storyboarding session, Mark felt that he had a clear plan of action and no longer felt overwhelmed. He felt renewed enthusiasm for his career choice and was eager to proceed.

STORYBOARDING YOUR FUTURE

Step 1: Start with a well formed outcome
- Use the outcome process to create a well formed outcome with clear guidelines for achievement. Storyboarding is best with long term outcomes (one year in this example).

Step 2: Storyboard the Outcome
- 1/2 point (6 months)
- For each step, get clear and strong evidence of movement toward the goal.

Step 4: 1/8 point (6 weeks)

Step 3: 1/4 point (3 months)

Step 5: current actions

Step 6: Connect the points
- Link the present to the future with an imaginary line that goes from client through all the points 1/2, 1/4, 1/8 to the outcome.

Step 7: Test
- Ask the client how the process has impacted their goal, goal clarity, and motivation.

STATE MANAGEMENT

What is it?

This is a process to be able to choose the state of mind that you want in any context. Many work challenges arise because people do not manage themselves well and act out of unresourceful states. Coaching employees to manage their own state empowers them to get better results on the job and in life.

Why use it?

- To be able to access and maintain the state of mind that is most useful for a specific context—examples of states include being accepting, articulate, relaxed, focused, playful, and so on.

- To increase flexibility and personal power.

- To manage yourself and maintain a resourceful frame of mind.

What does it do?

- Offers a powerful way of programming yourself now to automatically access the state when you want it.

- Allows you to identify a desired state for a particular context.

- Provides a method for accessing the desired state.

- Provides a means to maintain the state for the appropriate time.

- Describe the situation or context in which you want to access a certain state. Identify whether you want to succeed at a certain performance (for example, singing), to solve a problem (for example, working through a computer glitch), to deal with others (for example, resolving a problem with your boss), or to do a task (for example, writing a project plan). Identify who, what, where, and when. Consider the activities that go before and after the context.

- Identify the state of mind that would be appropriate or most powerful in the situation: playful, alert, flexible, and so on.

Consider the following:

- What are your goals and intents for your state in the situation?

- What evidence will let you know that you have accessed the desired state (breathing fully, smiling, staying focused, and so on)?

- What will you do to achieve and maintain the state (technique, posture, mental set, intent, and so on)? Consider several ways that you can maintain the state.

- What potential problems could arise that could throw you off in relation to your state? What will you do to regain it? Consider several ways to regain the state if you get thrown off.

Case Study 1

William was about to make a major sales presentation that could give him a hefty commission and add a significant contract to the company's book of business. He wanted to be at his best and chose this goal as the focus of a coaching session.

State management seemed an appropriate coaching tool for William's situation.

William described the context as the conference room at the host company. He had been there once before for a preliminary meeting and had met two managers that would be involved in the decision. The meeting would include these two managers, the CFO and the CEO of the company. This was clearly a "performance context."

Before the meeting, William would organize his materials and make sure that the PowerPoint presentation and other materials were in place and ready to go. He had arranged with the managers to arrive ten minutes early to set up everything in the conference room. After the meeting, he hoped to be celebrating a signed contract.

William's goal was to "wow" them. He intended to be upbeat, professional, enthusiastic, and fully prepared to handle any question that might arise. He noted that he was at his best when he adopted an attitude of detachment from the goal of making a sale, and instead focused on the people in the room and the moment. As evidence of this state, he imagined himself standing tall, feeling fluid in his body, and being mentally clear, focused, and upbeat.

When asked how he might achieve this state, William said that it helped to remember two things. First, he thought of his belief in his company and the product. Second, he thought of how he really likes people and that "high-level executives" are just people. When he focused on them as people, he felt connected to them, ready to hear what they had to say, and eager to make sure that they understood what he had to offer. He also felt less drive to "make the sale" and more confident that he could make the best presentation possible.

He felt that he could maintain the state by focusing on the process and the people, not on the end result. William came up with several methods to regain the confident state should he get thrown off, including a self-anchor for being present, use of his PowerPoint presentation as a process anchor, keeping his attention focused on the other people, and using the rapport that he had developed previously with the managers.

William's confidence seemed to grow with each answer to the state-management questions. At the end of the process, he was glowing, and said that he felt sure he could do his best. At the next coaching session, William reported that the officers did not sign the contract at the end of the meeting as he had hoped, but the state-management process worked beautifully, and he felt that he had done his best. He then announced that they had called two days later to negotiate the details and had signed the contract the next day!

Case Study 2

Fred was applying for a new position. Part of the application process included an interview with a panel of directors, and he was a bit nervous about this. Using the state-management process, Fred first thought through the context in detail. He identified the state that he wanted to be in during the interview. He wanted to be articulate, flexible, warm, and have a sense of conviction. He identified the physiological and mental evidence for each state. Then he decided how he would access the states.

He remembered times when he had been in each state. He mentally stepped back into the experience and relived it. He noticed his feelings and how his body felt during the experience. He noticed that if he stood up while doing this, it was easier to truly access the states.

He used appropriate language to help drive the states. For example, to access the state of conviction, he said, "I know that I know" in a convincing tone of voice. To elicit warmth, he imagined looking at each person on the panel and thinking, "I am glad you're here."

He found postures that supported each state and found ways to move his body to enhance the state congruently.

He then thought about what might happen that could throw him off balance: being asked tricky questions, rudeness on the part of a panel member, and so on. He then rehearsed dealing with strange questions or off-putting behavior until he was satisfied that he would maintain the state.

He later reported to his coach that the interview was a "breeze."

STATE MANAGEMENT

Step 1:
Specify the context

Describe the situation or context in which you want to achieve a certain state such as:

- Performing
- Problem solving
- Relating to others
- Accomplishing a task

Step 2:
Identify the desired state

- What is an appropriate, powerful state that supports effectiveness in the situation?

Step 3:
Considerations in identifying a state

- Goals and Intents: What is your goal in the situation?
- Evidence: How would you know you are in the desired state?
- Actions: What steps or actions can you take to initiate the state?
- Recovery: What can you do to recover the state if you get thrown off?

Techniques

APPRECIATIVE INQUIRY

Appreciative Inquiry (AI) is a new approach to personal and organizational development based on social constructionist theory. It states that human systems are made and imagined by those who live and work within them. AI has grown rapidly since its inception in 1987 from the work of David L. Cooperider, Ph.D., and Suresh Srivastva, Ph.D., from the Weatherhead School of Management at Case Western University.

Traditional change-management efforts are deficit-based and focus on fixing what is wrong, an approach that presupposes that there is something wrong with the system. AI is strength-based, and places the focus squarely on what is right and what is working within a system. The goal is to find what you appreciate, inquire into it, dialogue about it, and build on the positive core within a person or organization.

AI is both a perspective and a set of practices. It has been applied to organizational change with major corporations, systemic changes in social systems or groups, and to individual change.

People are more successful and live happier lives when they build on their strengths. The model of AI provides a basic framework for effective coaching because it identifies and builds on strengths. The basic idea is simple: find what you appreciate (a strength) and inquire into it. The format for the inquiry is to go backward, inward, and then forward.

Why use it?

- To bring the best of the past forward.
- To identify and build on strengths.

What does it do?

- Provides resources useful for specific situations.
- Provides a model for learning from experience.
- Offers a basic format for effective questioning in a coaching context (backward-inward-forward).

How do I do it?

- Identify something that you appreciate about yourself (an activity, a value, or a strength) or something that you appreciate in a system (a company activity, company values, or company strengths).

- Go backward. Recall a time when the activity, value, or strength was expressed. This process will be much more effective when you (or your client) recalls and relives an actual experience.

- Go inward. Inquire into the experience while the person relives it to identify the conditions and ingredients that made it work. Here are some questions to ask or areas to consider:

  #### CONDITIONS
  - What were the conditions in the environment that allowed the strength to be expressed?
  - What did others or the system do that helped to express the strength?

APPRECIATIVE INQUIRY

Step 1: Identify the appreciative topic
- Identify something about yourself or your company that you appreciate (activities, values, personal or company strengths).

Step 2: Backward
- Recall an actual expression of topic (activity, value, strength).

Step 3: Inward
- Relive the experience. Tell the story! And uncover:
- Conditions: what outer conditions contributed to the experience?
- Ingredients: What other ingredients helped? (your state of mind? Actions? Contributions?)
- Beliefs/Values: What beliefs and values did you operate on at that time?

Step 4: Forward
- Take the elements and ingredients uncovered in step 3 and bring them forward to the present or future situations.

INGREDIENTS

- What state of mind goes along with the strength?

- What was your goal?

- What did you do to express the strength?

- How did you do it?

- What ingredients contributed to expression?

BELIEFS AND VALUES

- What beliefs and values help to express the strength?

- What was your part in making it happen?

- Go forward. Take what is learned from going "inward," and bring these gifts forward into the present and the future. You can apply what is learned to almost any situation, and it does not need to be only for those situations where the strength "naturally" occurs. In fact, the conditions, ingredients, beliefs, values, and contributions provide much material that can be helpful (in surprising ways) in moving toward any goal or issue in a coaching context. Ask, "How can you use what you have learned here for (the goal or issue)?"

Case Study

Julie was stuck on a project at work; she had to roll out an in-house training academy. The project required collaborative teamwork with members of another department who were less invested in the project, and she was falling behind schedule. There was a history of strained relations between the two departments from before her tenure, and she felt some people were holding old grudges against her. She wanted to resolve the matter herself rather than take a complaint to her superiors.

Using AI, Julie recalled how she would get herself through the tough times by thinking about how amazing it would be if she pulled off a success despite the odds against her. After all, she had no staff, no real authority, and very few resources. She needed others to make projects happen, and they were already very busy with their own workloads.

Julie immediately realized that she had gotten caught up in the politics of the organization and had lost sight of the project vision. She had also avoided using her own manager because she feared that her concerns about the other department would be perceived as blame and would make a bad situation worse. Julie recognized direct parallels between the two situations and how she could use all that she had learned then to help her now.

Julie felt clear about what she needed to do. First, she needed to revitalize the vision of a superb training academy that would be a mark of distinction in the organization. She knew that she could formulate requests, incorporating the vision, in a way that would take some of the pressure off of others, making it easier to get them involved. She began feeling excited about "pulling it off" despite the history in the organization, and about how this achievement could really improve her job, and her perspective, overall.

GREGORY BATESON'S PROBLEM-SOLVING STRATEGY

What is it?

This technique, adapted by Robert Dilts from the work of Gregory Bateson, uses life experiences to solve problems or gain new perspective on difficult or challenging situations. It is unique in that the resources to solve a problem are obtained from a life experience that is totally unrelated to the challenge or difficulty. This new life experience is used to metaphorically frame the challenge and find creative solutions for the problem situation.

Why use it?

- To solve problems.

- To obtain perspective on difficult or challenging situations.

- To get out of or beyond "stuck states".

What does it do?

- Provides access to resources from the client's life experiences.

- Uses metaphor to discover creative solutions to challenges.

How do I do it?

This technique works best when you use "spatial anchoring." Spatial anchoring allows you to separate aspects or steps in the process by separating them in space. Create three physical locations in front of you and designate them as follows:

Problem State		Resource State
	Observer State	

1. Think of some problem with which you are at an impasse, such as an "inability to concentrate on studies."

2. Step into the Problem State location; associate into the problem situation and experience what is happening.

3. Step out of the Problem State and into the Observer State position.

GREGORY BATESON'S
PROBLEM-SOLVING STRATEGY

Step 1
- Identify a problem where you are "stuck" and not finding a ready solution.

Step 2
- Think of an activity or ability that you do that is completely unrelated to the current situation and which is a resource for you—something that really gives you a sense of identity, mission, creativity, or passion. Imagine doing this activity to bring forth the good feelings that derive from it.

Step 3
- Metaphorically, if the problem were being expressed in the context of the resource ability, what would be happening?

Step 4
- Find the solution to the problem from within the metaphor.

Step 5
- Translate and apply the metaphoric solution to the original context.

4. Think of something that you do that is completely unrelated to the problem situation and is a resource for you—an activity or ability (such as skiing) that really gives you a sense of identity, mission, creativity, passion, and so on.

5. Step into the Resource State location and associate into the resource experience.

6. Look over at the Problem State from the Resource State. Make a metaphor for the problem situation in the context of the resource activity. That is, if the problem were being expressed in the context of the Resource State, what would be happening? (An inability to concentrate is like constantly getting one's skis crossed.)

7. Find the solution to the problem from within the metaphor. (When you are getting your skis crossed, it is best to slow down, focus on moving one ski, and let the other ski follow.)

8. Step out of the metaphoric situation into the Problem State and bring the solution with you. Translate and apply the metaphoric solution to the original context. (When it is time to study, slow down, pick one thing to study, focus on it, and let the other things follow.)

Case Study

Larry had failed the bar exam on three separate occasions. He was scheduled to take the exam for the fourth time in a week. In his coaching session, he described how thoroughly he had studied and how well he had performed on the practice exams; he always scored well above passing level. But at test time, he would "lose it," become confused by the questions, and fail to finish in the allotted time.

Applying Bateson's Problem-Solving Strategy, Larry used his practice as a martial artist for a resource context. Considering the problem from this perspective, he realized that poor functioning in the test was like being too focused on yourself in sparring and not noticing your opponent. The solution in sparring was to focus on the opponent, trust your training, and let your responses come automatically.

He understood that the key was having a kind of panoramic view of the situation. When he took this idea into the Problem State, he imagined letting himself have his attention directed outward in a more panoramic view, and he instantly felt the feelings that he had when sparring. He immediately felt more relaxed and more capable of responding to test questions. One week later, Larry passed his exam.

NEW BEHAVIOR GENERATOR

Why use it?

New Behavior Generator was developed from modeling the mental processes that quick learners use to put new behaviors into their lives. It can also be used to create a new habit and immediately adopt it. Therefore, this is a great tool for coaching employees to create and implement new skills or behaviors on the job. When done properly, the client will automatically remember to use the new behavior; he should not have to consciously try to remember it.

What does it do?

This process uses mental imagery and rehearsal to quickly learn a new behavior. It allows one to "program one's self now" to automatically remember to do the new behavior later.

Here is an example. A client found herself getting involved in her e-mail when she first arrived at her office. She realized that when she did this, she tended to respond to e-mail, which took up her time and was not in alignment with her real priorities. Instead, she wanted a new habit of taking the time to plan her day in the morning before she did anything else. The New Behavior Generator helped her to install the new behavior in such a way that she remembered to do her planning first and felt motivated to continue to do so.

How do I do it?

1. Find a "stuck" situation where you are not as resourceful as you would like to be. Review it as if it were a movie that you were watching with you in it. Notice how you typically behave in that situation.

2. Find a resource state that might work better for you than what you are currently doing in the stuck situation. If you can't find a resourceful behavior that you have used in the past, either pretend that you can ("As If") or think of someone else who is resourceful and model them.

3. Review the stuck situation using the new behavior as if it were a movie that you were watching with you in it. If you like the way that it looks, go on to Step 4. If you don't like the way it looks, go back to Step 2 and find another resource that might work; then go on to Step 3.

4. Review the stuck situation using the new behavior as if you are actually experiencing it now. Jump into your body, into the movie, and experience it. If you like the way it feels, go on to Step 5. If you don't like the way it feels, go back to Step 2 and find another resource.

5. This step is to rehearse the new behavior so that it will be used in the future: Think of an external cue that will remind

NEW BEHAVIOR GENERATOR

Step 1 Identify a new habit or a behavior to change.

Step 2 Watch a movie of what your are currently doing.

Step 3 Identify a new behavior that works better
One you've done before (or)
Find a model who does it well (or)
Make it up.

Step 4 Watch a movie of yourself with this new behavior. If you like it, move to step 5.
If not, modify it until you do like it.

Step 5 Find a cue in the context to let you know when to do the new behavior.
Rehearse it if it feels right.

Step 6 Rehearse it in several contexts where you want it.

you to automatically use the new behavior in the kind of context where you would have been stuck in the past. Imagine that external cue (hearing something or seeing something in your environment) and feel yourself using the new behavior in that situation. Do it several times in several different contexts for excellent results.

Case Study

Fred had a hard time getting up in the morning. He would hear the alarm go off, but he would then push the snooze button, roll over, and go back to sleep. He continued to do this repeatedly until the last minute. He would then get up and rush around, often being late for meetings or arriving at work feeling frazzled.

He wanted to get up earlier and feel good about it, though he could not think of a time that he had ever done so as an adult. Since he did not have a past behavior to use, he thought of a friend who was "a real morning person" and who always arose easily. He asked her what she did. She was the kind of person who woke up early each morning, "leaping out of bed and ready to go."

In thinking it through, his friend realized that when she heard her alarm clock sound, she would say to herself, "It's time to get up." Then she would leap out of bed and stretch her arms. Fred thought this sounded like a good idea. Using the New Behavior Generator process, he ran a mental movie of sleeping in and pushing the snooze button repeatedly. Then he ran a movie of what he wanted to do instead. He saw himself lying in bed, hearing his alarm clock ring, and saying to himself, "It's time to get up." He then saw himself jump out of bed and stretch his arms. He liked the way that looked, so he tried it out as a rehearsal. He imagined being in that situation, hearing the alarm, and jumping up and stretching. His body said, "No way am I going to jump out of bed, first thing in the morning!" He then found a way to modify hearing the alarm and turning it off as he said, "Time to get up." Then he rehearsed slowly sitting up, getting up, and stretching. He felt that this would work much better for him. He rehearsed this process several times. He reported that the very next morning he had gotten up and stretched the first time that the alarm went off.

RESOURCE STATES

What is it?

We all experience times when we get "stuck" or respond poorly to life situations. This process allows you to gain a new perspective on situations that trigger ineffective reactions and provides you or your client with new choices and responses.

Why use it?

These resource strategies are widely applicable in lots of coaching situations and are especially useful for times when your client gets stuck (anxiety, anger, embarrassment, and so on) and is unable to respond appropriately and resourcefully.

What does it do?

The idea is to help the client to detach from the situation, gather her resources, and then step back into the situation with more resources. If done properly, the situation will change dramatically for the client.

These ideas are useful when the client identifies a situation in which being in a non-resourceful state prevents her from responding in the way that would be best for her.

- Isolate the situational trigger that initiates the non-resourceful state (words, tone, non-verbals, place, and so on). Have the client identify a specific example.

- Have the client mentally step into the situation at the point when she first realizes that she is having the undesired response.

- Have the client dissociate from the situation by having her take a deep breath and step back to watch herself in that situation. To create a greater sense of detachment, have the client imagine that she is watching herself through a thick Plexiglas window.

- Have her identify the most appropriate responses for the "you over there." Assist the client to build up a complete representation of this new response.

- Now have the client associate by stepping back into the situation with her new response. If a new response is needed or if adjustments need to be made in the selected response, repeat Steps 3, 4, and 5. Repeat Steps 1 to 5 as many times as is necessary to learn the strategy.

- Bridge the new behavior into the real world by rehearsing steps 1 to 5 with a future example.

- Test by directing the client to think of a future or past example of that context and calibrate for response.

RESOURCE STATES

Step 1 — Have the client mentally step into the situation at the point when he first realizes that he is having the undesired response.

Step 2 — Have the client dissociate from the situation by having him take a deep breath and step back to watch himself in the situation. To create a greater sense of detachment, have the client imagine that he is watching himself through a thick Plexiglass window.

Step 3 — Have him identify the most appropriate responses for the "you over there". Assist the client to build up a complete representation of the new response.

Step 4 — Now have the client associate by stepping back into the situation with her new response.

Step 5 — Bridge the new behavior into the real world by rehearsing the steps with a future example.

1. Have the client see the big picture from a distance ("the Jolly Green Giant" perspective).

2. If it is a still picture, make a movie out of it.

3. Freeze-frame the mental movie of the situation and then step out of it. Feel the resources and then step back into the scene.

4. Consider the situation from the perspective of ten years from now.

5. If appropriate, make some element of the situation incongruous—for example, have the person watch the situation from a distance and change the sound to puppies barking; put music behind the scene; run the situation at half speed and the client at double speed, popping them out at the end before the situation is over.

6. Anchor a state of inner peace and witness the situation, then step into it.

Case Study

Iris was dealing with a judgemental coworker and found herself avoiding this person, even though interfacing with him was necessary for her job. She remembered being with the difficult coworker earlier in the day, when she felt that the person repeatedly criticized her report at a staff meeting. She then mentally stepped back from the scene and went to an Observer position, watching herself at the meeting. This gave her the distance to add in new resources, which she did as described above. She tried out all of these new perspectives and reframes. (Note that you don't typically need to have the client do all of them; you might just select the one or ones that intuitively seem most likely

IDEAS FOR BUILDING MORE RESOURCEFUL STATES

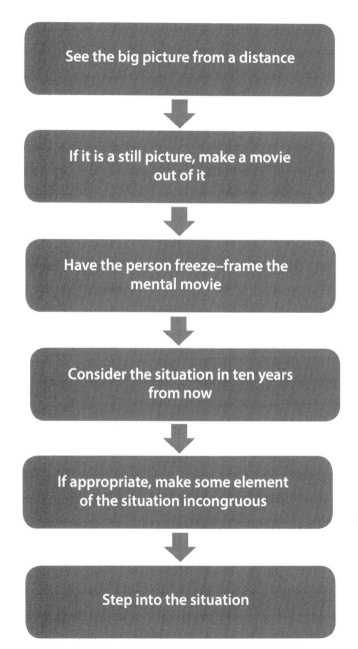

See the big picture from a distance

If it is a still picture, make a movie out of it

Have the person freeze–frame the mental movie

Consider the situation in ten years from now

If appropriate, make some element of the situation incongruous

Step into the situation

to make the greatest change.) Iris literally couldn't get her angry feelings back after adding these new resourceful ways of thinking. She later reported that her coworker had stopped criticizing her. She clearly was giving him something different to respond to while she was taking a new perspective on the situation.

Notice that the goal here is to empower the client, not to try to change the other person.

CREATIVE SOLUTION-FINDING PROCESS

REFRAMING AS A CONSCIOUS COACH PROCESS

What is it?

This process is designed to engage creative problem solving while respecting the ecology of the system. At some point, everyone faces the challenge of changing a limiting behavior: those things that we do but wished we didn't do. The coach can use this process to help employees address problem behaviors and create new, empowering choices that truly fit them, the company, and others that may be affected.

Why do it?

The process helps the client find creative solutions to problem behaviors that can be implemented with minimal inner or systemic resistance.

This process respects the fact that just about every problem behavior has a positive function supporting it, and it utilizes this idea to change the behavior while preserving the positive function. For example, smoking cigarettes might help a person relax. Quitting smoking is difficult because the person will lose a habitual way of relaxing. To effect the change, the person needs to find another way to relax that is just as immediate and as effective.

How to do it:

1. Identify the behavior to be changed. Reframing works best on a behavior that you do but don't want to do (being late, procrastinating about starting to do certain tasks, not completing projects or activities, and so on). Name the behavior.

   Explore the behavior to change and when and where it occurs. Get a clear sense of the "present state."

2. Separate the behavior from the positive intention. Find the meta-outcome of the problem behavior by asking, "What does doing that behavior or avoiding that activity get for you?" Ask this question several times until the benefit, the positive intention of the behavior, is identified.

3. Get agreement to try new choices. Ask, "If there were other actions that you could take, or other behaviors that you could do, that would work as well or better than what you are currently doing (to achieve the positive intention), would you be interested in discovering them?" (A "no" response indicates a misunderstanding, so restate the question.)

4. Create alternate behaviors to satisfy the intention.

   Help the client access a creative state and brainstorm at least three new ways to satisfy the positive intention. Check to make certain that the new choices are as immediate, powerful, and effective as the prior choice in achieving the goal.

5. Bridging the change into action.

   - Try out the new behaviors (in the imagination) in the appropriate future contexts to see how they might actually work.

- Ask the client or team if they are willing to take responsibility to actually do the new behaviors. Check to see if the client wants to be accountable, and if so, set up appropriate accountabilities.

- Ask, "Are there any possible downsides, concerns, or problems that might occur as a result of making these changes?

- If "yes," modify the new behavior until the concern is fully satisfied.

Case Study

George's work unit was experiencing a common problem: most of the staff arrived late to the weekly staff meeting. After repeated and fruitless requests for everyone to be on time, George followed the steps above for a resolution.

Most of the staff's positive intention was to avoid wasting time. If they arrived at the meeting at the last minute, then they felt they would not waste their time sitting around waiting for others to show up! Of course, the delay in getting the meeting going became longer and longer with this strategy, and the "solution" to the problem actually increased it and perpetuated it.

The group brainstormed and quickly arrived at a solution that was not only simple but actually worked for them. The meeting time was changed to the first moments of the day each Tuesday. The staff, for the most part, made the meeting the first activity of the day and did not get involved in anything else first.

CREATIVE SOLUTION FINDING:
REFRAMING

Step 1
- Identify behavior to be changed. Get a clear idea of the present state.

Step 2
- Ask "what will doing that get for you? This will identify the positive purpose of the behavior.

Step 3
- Gain agreement to consider new behaviors that will satisfy the positive purpose.

Step 4
- Help the client access a creative state and brainstorm new behaviors that willl satisfy the positive purpose.

Step 5
- Try out the new behaviors in your imagination in the appropriate future contexts to find out how they might work. If they look good - gain committment to do them.

Step 6
- Identify any possible downsides to employing the new behaviors. If yes, modify the new behaviors until they work.

GETTING CLEAR ABOUT CRITERIA

Adapted from Dan Thomas, Focus Inc. Work is largely a process of decisions and commitments. Many employees feel conflicted or make poor decisions about work situations because they have not clarified their own criteria. The coach can help the employee to determine what is truly important in a particular context, such as a work project or other situations, such as creating collaborative relationships with fellow employees.

Why use it?

- To make better choices and decisions within an area of life.

- To increase the likelihood of finding fulfillment in life.

- To improve quality of life.

What does it do?

- Clarifies what is important in a life context.

- Identifies specific criteria that may be used for decisions.

- Ensures criteria are properly sorted and ranked.

How do I do it?

Note about the words "criteria" and "values".

We evaluate the world and make choices based on what is important to us. Values and criteria are words used to express what is important. Both of these terms reflect what is important and there is some overlap between them.

Value words/phrases are more general and do not specify a behavior or condition. Values often go across contexts in life and can be applied in many situations. Values give direction and determine life satisfaction. For instance, you might value "freedom." But the meaning of freedom and how you determine this value is being met will likely differ in different contexts. Freedom in relationship to your spouse may be very different than freedom on a job.

Criteria words/phrases are usually more specific and are attached to a specific context. Criteria will provide a behavior or condition that you seek in a specific context. For instance, "flexible hours" may be a criterion for a job. Criteria provide a measure to determine whether a value is being met. "Flexible hours" may fulfill a value for "freedom" on the job. Criteria are used to help make decisions and to determine what is acceptable or unacceptable.

We title this exercise, "getting clear about criteria," because we are asking the client to consider a specific context or a role. Then we ask the person to identify what is important within that context or role. According to the above definitions, we are asking for criteria.

Step 1: Identify the Context

The context can be any part of one's life that needs clarification or improvement. This might be career, relationship, lifestyle, health, etc.

Step 2: Elicit the Criteria

Ask, "What's most important to you about _____ ?" (your career, your relationship, your role as manager, etc.)

Write person's answer in big letters on an 8 X 11" sheet of paper. (It is important to use the person's exact words.)

> Once you get the first answer, keep asking,

> "What else is important to you about _____?"

Keep asking until they run out of answers. A typical range is six to 12. Most people run out of criteria at a dozen.

Step 3: Rank the Criteria

Put the pieces of paper on the floor in the exact order in which the person identified them. Then ask them to arrange the pieces of paper from most important to least important:

> "Please arrange your criteria starting with the most important first, and the least important last."

Then it is very important to check the order.

Starting at the top of the list, have them stand beside the piece of paper and ask,

> "Is the most important thing about (this context) criteria #1 ?" (Actually name the criterion they have stated.)

If you get a "no" then ask what is most important and rearrange the pieces of paper.

If you get a "yes" then move them to stand beside #2.

Then, once they are beside #2, the language becomes very important. Preface this checking process by saying something like, "I know that what I am going to ask you next may sound unrealistic, but do your best to answer it and it will help you to rank your criteria."

"If you couldn't have #2, but could have #1, would that be okay with you?" Force it as an absolute—they have to choose one or the other. This forcing process will indicate which is really more important.

Your sensory acuity will tell you the answer long before the client verbalizes it. If the answer is "yes," move on down the list. If the answer is "no," switch the pieces of paper and ask the question again. (NOTE—If they cannot congruently answer the question, then there is some additional value. (It may be one in the list, but often is something that they didn't consciously articulate yet.)

Once the ranking is clarified, move on to the other criteria:

> "Assuming you have the criteria already chosen (i.e. #1), if you couldn't have #3, but could have #2, would that be okay?"

> Repeat this process until the list is rank ordered.

Step 4: Check for Missing Criteria

Once you have gotten the person's list in rank order, do a check for logic. You may find criteria missing. For example, if we are doing, "What is important to you about your business?" And "making money," "getting wealthy" or something related is not there, there is likely a criteria missing.

> Say something like, "This is a terrific list of criteria. However, I am curious about something. This list is about your business and yet I don't see anything here about making money."

Step 5: Moving criteria up and/or installing new criteria

Once the "Present State" has been elicited, we know "what is." It will often be the case that it is obvious to the client that the ranking is not serving him/her well, and is the source of some difficulty.

Ask, "Is there anything you would like to change about this list of criteria?"

The client may want to change the ranking, and/or install a new value if they have discovered one that is missing.

Experience indicates that: (1) typically, only the top three or four criteria provide substantial motivation toward action, and (2) the client and the coach need to have a VERY good reason to change a person's #1 value. Changing #1 will change a person's life. As always, be careful about the potential negative impacts of change.

Step 6: Cementing the new hierarchy

Once the new or reshuffled value is in the hierarchy, have the client associate into (step into) his/her highest value and anchor them there. Then have them step backward, using appropriate language, such as, "And your highest criterion of _____ will be supported by your criterion of _____. "

Coach has the client walk all the way down the hierarchy. Then have them step all the way out of the hierarchy and check for congruency, ecology, appropriateness, etc.

Finally, start them at the lowest criterion and walk them UP the hierarchy, taking each lower criterion with them to support the next higher one. It is important to end with them fully associated to their highest criterion and all the supporting criteria.

Case Study

Marjorie described ongoing tension between her young adult son, Brian, and her husband, Tom, which caused her and her daughter a great deal of strain. She emphasized that she really wanted them to resolve their differences, come together, and restore family harmony. The holiday season was approaching and she dreaded the thought of conflict during that time of year.

GETTING CLEAR ABOUT CRITERIA

Step 1
- Identify the context where clarifying criteria is useful. (Buying a house)

Step 2
- Elicit the client's criteria: What is most important about "X" context? "What is next most important?" and so on. (Collect 6 to 12 criteria)

Step 3
- Rank the criteria by forced choice method: if you could have criteria #1 without #2, would it be OK?

Step 4
- Check for missing criteria by asking the client the criteria if anything is missing or by pointing out what might be missing.

Step 5
- Ask if the client wants to change the order or add missing criteria and re-rank accordingly. Usually, the top 3 or 4 are most important in decision making

Step 6
- "Anchor" the new hierachy by reviewing and intergrating the new order

We used the criteria process to explore what is important to her with family. She listed a variety of criteria, including harmony, togetherness, sharing, supporting each other, etc. She completed her list, writing each one on a card and laying them out in an initial order on the floor. The value of harmony came out on top when she went through the process of ranking them.

Marjorie realized that this value was so important to her that she had difficulty seeing beyond it. She felt excessive strain because she was "over-emphasizing" this one criterion and neglecting others. This insight alone began to put things in perspective for her.

I asked her to step back to consider if any important criterion was missing. I knew Marjorie to be a gentle person who valued love, but she did not include love on her list and I pointed this out to her. She was immediately clear that it not only had a place, but was the top criterion. After adding this to the set and resorting it, she felt a tremendous feeling of relief about her family members. She again noted that she had been too focused on family harmony and now realized that she had neglected the overarching criterion of love.

With this insight, she was able to drop some of her anxiety about disharmony in the family and recognize the love that existed despite the differences. She realized that she had been "nagging" both her husband and Brian to resolve the problem between them. Marjorie later reported that she spoke with both of them and told them that she would love them both no matter what their differences. Within a few weeks, the atmosphere in the family lightened up quite a bit. Brian noted the change and told her that he had actually stayed away as much because he felt as much pressure from her as from the difficulty with his father.

DISNEY STRATEGY

(Developed by Robert Dilts)

The Disney Strategy is a pattern for generating creativity modeled from the work of Walt Disney by Robert Dilts, one of the co-founders of NLP. The strategy is based on the ability to enter three separate states: the Dreamer, the Realist, and the Critic. Each state will have a distinct physiology or posture, patterns of thought, and feelings.

Why use it?

- To learn and use a very creative strategy for success.
- To create clear goals or to turn dreams into reality.
- To plan clear steps to achieving goals.
- To ensure that goals meet specified criteria.
- To evaluate one's plan to make certain it is what you want and the downsides have been considered.

What does it do?

- Provides a clear strategy for goal-setting and planning.
- Clearly distinguishes the functions for effective creativity.
- Provides a method for evaluating and refining goals.

Role	Mindset	Activities
Dreamer	This is the state of mind in which you dream of possibilities.	The Dreamer is concerned with what "could be" or what you "could do" and not with what you "should do" or "must do" or even "will do." For most people, the Dreamer involves creating visual images, and often includes a feeling of excitement about new possibilities.
Realist	This is the state for creating plans and identifying steps to accomplish a goal.	The Realist is concerned with how to make something work and not whether it will work, or whether it is worth doing. The Realist identifies steps to accomplish the dream.
Critic	This is the state for evaluating the plan in relation to the outcome.	The goal of the critic is to find flaws in the plan, or missing pieces, and to determine if the plan really gets to the goal or meets the goal criteria. The Critic does not identify remedies. Disney stated that it was important to "get enough distance" from the plan to really think critically about it. This also helps to avoid criticizing yourself or other people.

DISNEY STRATEGY

Step 1
- Identify the goal or desired state.
- The Disney Strategy helps create a more robust and complete outcome. It can be used during or after the process of creating a well formed outcome.

Step 2 — The Dreamer Role
- Step into the Dreamer Role and vividly imagine the goal with all its benefits and possibilities.
- The dreamer is the big-picture visionary concerned with what is possible.

Step 3 — The Realist Role
- Step into the Realist Role and create plans and strategies to make the dream a reality.
- The realist is like an engineer concerned with how to make it happen.

Step 4 — The Critic Role
- Step back from the dream and enter the role of the critic, sorting for gaps in the plan or mismatches with the criteria the dream is supposed to fulfill.

Step 5
- If necessary, recycle back to step 2.
- Use information from the Critic Role to cycle back through to steps 2 – 5, repeating these steps until the critic is satisfied or there is enough of a plan to proceed.

1. Identify a goal or desired outcome.

2. Become the dreamer—your goal is only to generate possibilities in relation to the goal.

3. Take one of the possibilities and adopt a realist mentality. (Like a time when you planned something out successfully.) Your goal here is to identify the steps to realize the dream.

4. Step back from the plan.

5. Determine whether the plan really gets to the goal and is in line with your criteria, personal values, etc.

6. Take the information generated by the Critic and recycle through steps 2 through 4 until you are comfortable that you have enough of a plan to take action.

Case Study

Denise was charged with producing the annual company party, a special occasion during this particular year because the company founder was also retiring. They management team wanted the retirement celebration to be a surprise. They gave her a budget amount, some general guidelines, and asked her to come up with a basic plan for consideration by the team. Denise brought this matter to the coaching session and we used the Disney Strategy to help her develop a response.

With the party goal in mind, Denise stepped into the Dreamer position. She generated several options for location and party themes. The idea that appealed to her most was a Hawaiian/golf theme since the founder loved to golf and enjoyed Hawaii. She dreamed that the party could actually be in Hawaii, but knew this was not within the budget. However, what she did imagine was a lively event, filled with fun activities. She saw a "sand beach" with lawn chairs as the platform/stage where the founder would be toasted and his work celebrated. She saw a room decorated with Hawaiian images and a luau-style party with Hawaiian delicacies.

She took this option to the Realist position. Here she began to consider what was required to make such a party happen. She listed several specific steps, including:

- Research hotel sites or conference locations that could accommodate 300 staff and other "retirement surprise" visitors, and be within budget.
- Research catering of a luau-style party.
- Recruit help in decorating the site for the Hawaii theme.
- Find the decorations and stay within budget.
- Decide and coordinate party activities.
- Establish ways to inform everyone about the "retirement surprise" while keeping it a secret.

She took this plan to the Critic, stepping back from the idea to evaluate it, determine if the plan was complete enough to proceed, and whether or not it really met the criteria for the dream. From this position, she immediately realized the plan over-emphasized the retirement and did not take into account the annual party need. Plus, the plan was missing references to golfing.

She took this concern back to the Dreamer to generate options to combine the two needs. She revisited her original vision and considered several options: one was to start the party with the annual events and then bring in the surprise after a period. She imagined a screen or curtain, which would open to reveal the golf/Hawaii platform. The platform would include some sand beach, with a golf hole/flag, golf bags, and lawn chairs.

Cycling this back through the Realist, she identified the steps necessary to make this modification happen, including getting the sand, chairs, golf accessories, etc., which she knew would all be available from employees or family members.

The Critic wanted to fill in additional information about the actual activities especially related to the retirement portion. She took this to the Dreamer and imagined a "This is Your life" type of game, where people from his past would talk about his life. He would have to guess who they were based on a few clues before they came out. The Realist identified specific people from his past and present that might participate and how they could set it up.

The final adjustment offered by the Critic was how to present this to the management team. Taking this through the three positions, she decided to create a "storyboard" of the party, in honor of Walt Disney. The idea and plan was a hit with the management team, who offered full support and even extended the budget slightly based on her additional research regarding costs.

BELIEFS

(This section is influenced by the work of NLP Developer Robert Dilts)

What is a belief?

A belief is the acceptance of something as true, or thinking that something could be true. Beliefs are essentially judgments and evaluations about ourselves, about others, and about the world around us. All of us have empowering beliefs as well as limiting beliefs. Most of our influential beliefs are outside of conscious awareness and have a huge impact on our daily thoughts, actions, and general life experience.

DEFINITION:

NOUN:

1. The mental act, condition, or habit of placing trust or confidence in another: My belief in you is as strong as ever.

2. Mental acceptance of and conviction in the truth, actuality, or validity of something: His explanation of what happened defies belief.

3. Something believed or accepted as true, especially a particular tenet or a body of tenets accepted by a group of persons.

ETYMOLOGY: Middle English bileve, alteration (influenced by bileven, to believe), of Old English gelafa.

SYNONYMS: belief, credence, credit, faith. These nouns denote mental acceptance of the truth, actuality, or validity of something: a statement unworthy of belief; an idea steadily gaining credence; testimony meriting credit; has no faith in a liar's assertions. See also synonyms at opinion. *Definition from the American Heritage Dictionary® on-line at Yahoo.com reference page.*

We create our experience of life through our beliefs. The beliefs that we hold can shift as we learn new things and encounter new experiences, but often we hold them in a steady way and don't change them. Beliefs give us permission about what we can do and consider.

As Jan Elfline, Master Certified Coach, states: "As you work with clients, the first step is to make them aware that they have beliefs. This may sound absurd, but our beliefs are often invisible to us. We don't recognize our assumptions as beliefs. Instead, we think and feel they are simply descriptions of the way the world works. They go unquestioned and unexamined. In fact, we easily confuse our beliefs with "reality." Beliefs may be based on some evidence and may reflect some aspect of "reality," but they are still a just a map or a model of reality. We tend to follow only the path our beliefs allow and neglect the fact that the world is often richer and more varied than our beliefs permit us to see."

As your clients begin to be sensitive to how much of their thinking is driven by the beliefs they hold, they will choose to shape beliefs that will serve them. This may lead to a discussion about how beliefs are changed.

In *Beliefs: Pathways to Health and Well-Being*, the authors (Robert Dilts, Suzi Smith, and Tim Hallbom) tell the story of a man who believes he is a corpse. On several visits, his psychiatrist attempts to convince him that he is in fact alive, but to no avail. Finally the psychiatrist asks, "Do corpses bleed?" The man replies that of course corpses do not bleed, all of the systems in the body have stopped. The psychiatrist proposes an experiment. He will prick the man's finger with a needle. When he does and the patient starts to bleed the patient looks astounded and says, "I'll be damned, corpses do bleed!"

This story illustrates a point about beliefs and evidence. Beliefs are rarely changed by our experience of contradictory evidence. People generally choose to consider only the evidence that supports beliefs, or as the story illustrates, actively distort evidence to support beliefs. If someone has low self-esteem, no external acknowledgment will make him or her feel worthy. If someone thinks of him/herself as incompetent, no number of degrees and credentials will convince them that they are capable.

As a coach, you can work at the levels of behavior and capability, and there can be great value for the client in making changes at those levels. But at times even after desired behavioral changes have stabilized, the client does not experience the benefits they expected as a result of those changed behaviors. The behavior has changed, but old beliefs are still running the show.

In contrast, when beliefs begin to transform, desired and lasting behavioral changes come about with less effort. As an old belief shifts, changing what we do seems natural, and even inevitable. The old behaviors produce a feeling of incongruence. The new actions reflect current beliefs and "feel right."

In coaching you will have opportunities to address both beliefs about capabilities and beliefs about identity. From about the age of five onward, we develop skills and capabilities consciously by choosing what we learn. As we continue to grow, our beliefs about our capabilities expand. Children rarely question whether or not they are capable of doing something. They just try it. If they fail, they try again or in a different way. But as we grow older, we may try something several times, but when frustration sets in, we often assume that we are not capable and we never try again. As a coach, you may want to question the old evidence the client is referencing; how did they come to this belief about their capability?

As adults, we have little tolerance for moving through learning curves; and we get easily frustrated, and jump to conclusions about our capabilities. Albert Bandura at Stanford University studied how learning takes place and created the now famous Bandura Curve. He found that learning is a process of moving through crisis points. To progress, we must believe we can change or improve. As we believe in our capabilities, our performance rises to meet the belief. As we question our ability, our performance falters.

In working with clients, it is useful to assume that learning and change are processes that are influenced by our underlying beliefs. As coaches, we often speak about the processes of learning and change. We identify a dip as what it is, a stumble, not evidence that the client should quit striving for what they want.

Beliefs about identity often show up in the coaching relationship as "I am" statements. The client just assumes that "this is the way I am." Here again, the coach can challenge the client by suggesting that their statement is a belief. The coach could suggest that the client "try on" a different belief about who they are, and notice what behaviors would follow from the new belief.

People often have a sense that change at the identity level is difficult or even impossible. In reality, we are constantly in the process of inventing ourselves. By deciding to work with a coach, the client has chosen to be conscious about the process of defining what their life will be like. In essence, they are inventing a new identity for themselves. Your coaching questions can help them shape the new identity they want to live into.

Beliefs are central to an effective coaching relationship. You will achieve limited success with private individuals or in businesses if you do not invite your clients to look at their beliefs.

LIMITING BELIEFS

Beliefs can empower you or limit you. They can give you the courage to tackle what others say is impossible or make you feel something is impossible no matter what others say. Helping clients to identify limiting beliefs is one of the most valuable skills in coaching. Fortunately, limiting beliefs tend to fall into four categories:

1. Beliefs about Cause

These are beliefs about causal sources of events and experiences. Often these beliefs have the word "because" in them. Some examples of limiting beliefs about cause include:

- I can't be successful because my parents weren't successful.

- I don't deserve to have what I want because I am a woman.

- Life is a struggle because I never get what I want.

- We're not suppose to have money because we grew up poor.

- Money causes pain.

- Being successful will cause the family to split up.

2. Beliefs about Meaning

Beliefs can also be about meaning. As human beings we are always trying to find the meanings in things. For example, what does it mean that we are poor, or that we are rich; what exactly is the deeper meaning behind these things? The meanings that we put on these beliefs will guide our behavior, because they operate as filters for our belief systems. Some examples of limiting beliefs about meaning include:

- You did not respond to my hello and that means you don't like me.

- Money is the root of all evil.

- Taking time off means you're a slacker.

- Feelings are unimportant at work.

- Being late means you don't care about your job.

Beliefs can also be about possibility—what is possible, or not possible, for us. There are two kinds of beliefs about possibilities:

- **The outcome is perceived as possible:** If it is possible, then the person has permission from their unconscious mind to go for it.

- **The outcome is perceived as impossible:** If it is impossible, then the person will not even bother trying to get what they want. For example, if you believe that you can't get ahead because the economy is bad, and you hold that belief firm in your mind, then you won't do what it takes to be successful. You will give up ahead of time, and not do anything to create what you want. Some examples of limiting beliefs about possibility include:

  - I don't have the magic ingredient that is necessary to be successful.

  - Money is hard to manage. (I can't manage money.)

  - I don't know how to make money.

  - Large sums of money are for other people. (It isn't possible for me to have money.)

  - How to make money is a giant mystery.

  - If I make money, I will mess it up and lose it all.

  - I will never be rich.

The Power of Beliefs: Until May 6, 1954, it was assumed that to run a mile in less than four minutes was impossible. In the nine years prior to the day that Roger Bannister broke the four minute barrier, no one else had even approached the time. Bannister surpassed the four-minute-mile barrier because he knew it was possible and that he could do it. Within a few weeks after

Bannister's accomplishment, John Lundy from Australia lowered the record by another second. In the next nine years nearly two hundred people ran a mile in less than four minutes! The world no longer believed it to be impossible.

4. Beliefs about Identity

Beliefs that involve identity are about our worthiness about whether we deserve to attain wealth and success. Some examples of these kinds of limiting beliefs include:

- I am not good enough to be successful.

- I don't deserve to have what I want.

- I am not smart enough to make money.

- I don't have the right to live.

- I am not worthy of success.

- Nobody likes me, I am a loser.

Limiting beliefs tend to generate specific kinds of feeling states. When you encounter one of the following three feelings, you can be sure you are on the trail of a limiting belief:

1. **HOPELESSNESS** - Belief that the desired goal is not achievable, regardless of your capabilities. There is no hope that you will get what you want, because it is not really possible.

2. **HELPLESSNESS** - Belief that the desired goal is possible, but you are not capable of achieving it. You are helpless, and incapable of getting what you want.

3. **WORTHLESSNESS** - Belief that you do not deserve the desired goal because of something about you or because you are a "bad" person. Worthlessness may also arise because of a belief that you did or didn't do something that makes you worthless or undeserving.

WHAT IS A STEM BELIEF?

A stem belief is a powerful underlying belief that holds together a cluster of supporting beliefs. Metaphorically, changing a stem belief is incredibly powerful because when you do so all of the supporting beliefs fall off "the grapevine" of limiting beliefs. The reason why it can be challenging to change a belief is because most people only work with the individual "supporting belief" instead of the entire belief vine, or cluster of beliefs.

It can be difficult to permanently change a belief without getting to the core of the belief. This is why affirmations do not work sometimes. They typically do not address the stem belief; they only address one of the smaller, less charged beliefs.

Most stem beliefs are formed when we are small children. They often sound childlike in nature and can be simply stated. They can be difficult to find. However, with the right questioning, they can also be easily identified. Usually a person will get emotional, or even cry, when they become conscious of their stem belief for the first time.

Once they acknowledge the stem belief and get past the emotion of recognizing it, they can begin the process of healing and transforming it. The success rate for changing beliefs is incredibly high when you focus on identifying and changing the stem belief—because the stem belief holds together the whole cluster of related beliefs.

The most common stem beliefs that we have come across in our travels are:

- You have to work hard to make money.
- I'm not good enough to have what I want.
- I don't deserve to have what I want.
- Others come before me.
- I don't exist, I don't have the right to be here.

Questions and statements that help the client to examine beliefs:

- What is true about this?
- Is that a belief?
- You could choose to believe that.
- That is one perspective.
- Do you have a belief about what "should be" in this situation?
- There's a belief.
- And there's another belief. (This could go on for an entire call!)

BELIEF CHANGE PROCESS

(Adapted from a technique developed by Jan Elfline)

A simple belief change exercise involves heightening the client's awareness of a belief and the cluster if thoughts, feelings, and actions that surround it. Completing the following belief examination chart can often clarify what is at stake in holding a belief and stimulates desire to update and change beliefs.

Belief	Other Beliefs	Results
Belief	If this is true, what else must be true?	If all this is true, what actions will I take or not take?

Case Study

Angie had worked hard to attain a level of success in the high-tech industry. She managed a small group of engineers and computer-design specialists on a variety of projects. Yet she was unhappy with her career path. She had seen less qualified and less talented men receive promotions over her and felt she had been actively thwarted in her career advances. This topic came up on several occasions during our coaching work and she seemed ready to address the beliefs and ideas that she held in regard to these experiences.

I challenged Angie to consider that at least some of her experience resulted from her beliefs. At first, she thought this idea absurd because she had so much evidence that she had hit a "glass ceiling." I asked her to tell me what conclusion she derived from these experiences and she said, "Women are second-class." We used this statement as a basis for completing the belief examination chart. Her assignment was to do her best to thoroughly complete the boxes on the chart.

Belief	Other Beliefs	Results
"Women are second-class"	Men are first class; they will get more money and prestige for the same or even less work	Lots of resentment and anger, especially toward my boss
	Women will always be treated as less worthy	A sense of resignation and a feeling of being stuck--I have given up on pursuing promotions
	Women have to work harder to prove themselves	Occasional commiseration with a couple of women colleagues, which usually just depresses me
	I have to work harder because I am a woman	Often driven to do my best to show that I can perform as well or better than a man
	I have to be tougher than a man because any waffling on decisions is seen as my emotions getting in the way	Occasionally complain to management about being held back; once formally complained but it led nowhere
	Men will be given the credit for my accomplishments	Feeling that I am under appreciated and unrecognized

As Angie completed the chart, she became increasingly aware that her belief was itself causing her a lot of stress. We discussed the hopelessness she had developed because she believed that career advances were impossible for her as a woman. This provided an opportunity for coaching around this result.

Our first step was to examine what this chart revealed that is important to her. Angie said it was most important that she be recognized and appreciated for her work. We discussed how she first needed to learn to "toot her own horn" in an appropriate way and at appropriate times.

I gave her the task of completing a list of her accomplishments on the job and how these had impacted the company. She kept a running list over a two-week period, completing several pages of accomplishments. In the process, she talked with some colleagues and co-workers who also gave her insight into her contributions and the impact they had on them and on the company.

This exercise boosted her confidence considerably. Angie commented, "I was so caught up in feeling unappreciated that I neglected to appreciate what I had done myself."

Moreover, she felt less "edgy" when talking with her boss. Over the next few weeks, she began inserting references to her accomplishments at appropriate times in the conversation. She was shocked to hear her boss agree with her about one particular accomplishment. This made her realize that she had been silently waiting to be acknowledged rather than actively promoting herself.

Angie decided to take her whole list of accomplishments in to the boss. Her approach was to give him the list and say she felt like she could do so much more for the company, and to ask him where she might apply her talents. Again, she was surprised when he revealed a couple of upcoming opportunities that might be suited for her. Angie reported that, in the past, she would have only heard about these kinds of opportunities after someone else, a man of course, would be given them.

As we reviewed what had happened, Angie said she still believed that there was definite discrimination against women. But she realized that she had unwittingly colluded in the discrimination by operating on her belief about it in an unexamined way. She now felt much more comfortable with her own accomplishments, regardless of how much the world noticed. She felt more confident promoting herself and she believed it was more likely that she would find new opportunities either within her current company or by looking elsewhere.

IMPORTANT COACH REFLECTIONS

One of the Seven Habits of Highly Effective People, according to the classic work of Stephen Covey, is to "sharpen the saw." He uses the old metaphor of loggers competing in a log-cutting contest. One works without taking a break and jumps out to an early lead over the second, who stops periodically to sharpen his saw. Over time, however, the one who works without stopping must work harder because the blade dulls and cuts inefficiently. The second, who keeps the blade sharp, expends less energy and eventually overtakes the first, winning the contest. Successful people take the time to step back, review their own skills, and work to improve them. This process helps the coach to "sharpen the saw." This process is very important for the coach-manager, who can use the reflection to help keep roles clearly defined.

Why use this process?

- To sharpen your skills as a coach.
- To coach yourself.

What does it do?

- Encourages taking time to periodically reflect on your coaching process.
- Provides questions for reflection about how you conduct your coaching.
- Reminds you about specific principles of excellent coaching.

How do I do it?

This reflection process guides you through a series of questions that you can ask yourself for continuous improvement of your coaching skills. Take some time every month or two to answer these questions. Be specific in your answers. Use your actual experience and answer fresh each time. It is best to use this tool immediately after a coaching session or set of sessions.

- How do you know when you are doing a good job as a coach? What is your evidence?
- How do you know when your client feels really listened to?
- What is your sensory-based evidence that you are listening to your client?
- How do you know when you are making a positive difference with your client? What is your evidence for this?
- How do you hold back from giving information or offering a solution that you think would be helpful to your client (because you know that the best solution will be the one that you draw out from your client)?

- For coach-managers, how do you distinguish your roles as coach and manager? What has worked to help keep the roles clear?

- How do you manage and maintain your state as a coach?

- How do you use powerful questions with your client? What coaching crafts do you use? How do you use them?

- What is your "growing edge" as a coach?

After a few reflections, look over your answers and see if you notice patterns. Do you have challenges holding back advice? Are you using only a select set of coaching crafts? What throws you off track in your coaching, and how to do you get back on track?

Coaching is a way to help your clients live more consciously and deliberately. We should expect no less of ourselves as coaches!

PUTTING IT ALL TOGETHER

Coaching is one of the fastest growing professions because it works to help people achieve their goals. Work is largely a process of setting and accomplishing goals through individual and cooperative effort. Coaching draws out the strengths within people and allows them to grow and develop themselves, tap inner wisdom and motivation, and keep on track to realizing their dreams. Therefore, it is a perfect tool for the workplace and for encouraging employees to be at their best.

This book offers an overview of the coaching process and provides lots of tools to put coaching into practice. Although these tools can be used in any coaching relationship, we've focused on coaching employees in an organization. It is important to remember that coaching is primarily a relationship with defined roles and a focus on helping the client to achieve her goals.

Clarity regarding the roles of the coach and client is especially critical when the coach is also a manager with authority over a client (and, to a lesser degree, when the coach is also an employee of the same organization). These dual roles present challenges in creating a powerful coaching relationship, but it can be accomplished if the manager-coach is willing and able to step into the role of a coach. This means that the manager must allow the employee to define the coaching goals and take the lead in the coaching process.

Though this may be difficult at times, the rewards are well worth the effort. Coaching empowers employees, leads to increased motivation, enhanced performance, and heightened job satisfaction. Happier, more capable employees get more done and have better workplace relationships. Ultimately, this makes the job of managing easier! And you will be surprised how much you will learn from your "client" when you coach them to find their own solutions and create their own path.

Resources

INTERESTING ARTICLES

WONDERFUL LIFE PROCESS
Picture Your Life • Identify Values • Wonderful Life

HOW MANAGERS CAN USE COACHING SKILLS
by Tim Hallbom and Ashley Warrenton Smith

BRINGFORTHISM AND THE ART OF CREATING YOUR IDEAL FUTURES
by Kristine Hallbom

MEET THE AUTHORS:
Tim Hallbom and Nick LeForce

"Wonderful Life" Process

In life, it's sometimes useful to get the big picture. The following process allows you to step back, consider all life areas, and create a sense of overall fulfillment about your life as a whole.

Here's the process:

PHASE I: PICTURE YOUR LIFE AS A WHOLE

1. Identify the areas of your life.

2. Specify the top values for each area.

3. Identify evidence for value fulfillment.

4. Create goals based on value evidence.

Note: Use the "Picture Your Life" circle on the next page to come up with life areas.

PHASE II

5. Imagine manifesting values in selected area of life.

6. Create iconic representation of area of life as fulfilled.

7. Repeat with each area.

Note: Use the form "Identify Values" to come up with values for each area. I suggest picking the top three values in each area and then identifying the evidence (what you would see, hear, or feel) that each of those values fulfilled.

PHASE III:

8. Combine icons into a vision of your whole life fulfilled.

9. Associate into vision as if these icons surround you.

10. Future-pace: Envision a specific time in the future with your whole life fulfilled.

11. "As-If": Imagine your life now as if it were fulfilled, using your icons to help.

Note: You can also find actual images from magazines or the internet that reflect fulfillment in each area and paste them onto a poster board to create a vision map.

Picture Your Life

INSTRUCTIONS:

- Write "my life" in the center circle.
- Group related areas together.
- Draw lines and arrows to show relationships.
- Have fun.

Neatness is not important.

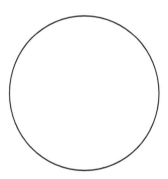

Identify Values

Pick one area of life to work on.

Work with a partner and interview each other.

What do you want in _____(name area of life)?

_____

What is important to you about _____(name area of life)?

_____

If you could have what you want in this area of life, what would that do for you?

_____

IDENTIFY EVIDENCE

Circle the top three value-words or phrases for this area of your life. For each value word or phrase, identify your evidence that the value is fulfilled. Partners do this with one value-word/phrase.

How would you know that _____(value) is happening?

_____

What are some indicators to you that _____ (value) has been achieved or fulfilled?

_____

Iconic Representation

1. Iconic Representation

   For each area of your life, create a symbol or an icon that represents the area of life as fulfilled. To do this, imagine you are living the top values you identified and that you are experiencing a moment of total satisfaction with the area of life. Now identify an image or symbol that captures this sense of fulfillment. Many people use images or symbols from nature, such as a sunrise or a fruit tree, or an "archetypal" symbol, like a sailboat or a lantern. Create a label for the icon or symbol.

   Area of Life: Icon or symbol

2. Combine the icons into a single coherent image that represents all areas of your life fulfilled and in balance with each other.

3. Imagine associating into the combined images as if they are around you and in you, as you go through life.

For example, one client had the image of the sun shining in a blue sky for the "spiritual" area of life, a fruit tree in blossom for the "career" area, his family together for a picnic for "family," a book for "learning," a postcard to represent "travel and recreation," and a pot of gold for "finances." He combined these into a scene of the family having a picnic under the tree on a sunny day with several postcards spread on the table next to a book. He imagined a beautiful rainbow across the sky that ended on a pot of gold near the tree.

How Managers Can Use Coaching Skills

BY TIM HALLBOM & ASHLEY WARRENTON SMITH

We interviewed successful managers who ranged from chairmen and CEOs to front-line managers, from companies ranging from start-ups to Fortune 50. We asked them to identify the challenges they faced in obtaining high performance from direct reports; how they currently coach direct reports to achieve higher performance; what coaching meant to them; whether they had ever been coached and, if so, what worked for them about it; and skill sets that managers need to be effective at coaching. Finally, we asked if most of the managers they worked with had the skill sets they needed to coach effectively. Here are some of their recommendations.

1. Ask high-impact questions that draw out the highest and best thinking in your direct reports to help them develop their own answers and move them to action.

2. Focus upon what is working rather than trying to "fix problems."

3. Stay focused on the results you want.

4. Build rapport and trust—make it safe for reports to speak their minds.

5. Hold your direct reports accountable. You get what you expect.

6. Listen deeply with your eyes, ears, and heart.

7. Model what you desire from your direct reports. Walk your talk.

These bullet points are from an article we wrote for the *Journal of Innovative Management* .

"Bringforthism" and the Art of Creating Your Ideal Future

BY KRISTINE HALLBOM

You are always creating your future. You bring it forth through your thoughts, actions, feelings, beliefs, values, goals and dreams. You do this regardless of the level of your conscious awareness. Your present moment awareness coupled with the future that you create is a deeper reflection of your subconscious programming. We will call this way of creating your life experience "bringforthism." [1]

Understanding the key elements of bringforthism allows you to more "consciously" create the future that you want, versus "unconsciously" creating the future that you don't want. [2] Intentionally using the concept of bringforthism is a powerful approach to take in achieving any of your goals or future dreams. Once you recognize how your mind really works, it becomes more possible to achieve almost any goal.

For example, when Tiger Woods, the great American golfer, was a little boy, he wrote down all of his golfing goals on a piece of paper. Every night before he went to bed, he looked at his goals and thought about what it would be like to be the greatest golfer in the world. He then unconsciously stepped into his future by imagining what it would be like to break all the greatest golfing records in history.

Tiger firmly set his intent to make this goal happen, while pretending that it had already happened in his subconscious mind's eye. He then put all of his conscious attention on achieving the goals that he wrote down as a boy. As a result of doing this,

Tiger developed a deep subconscious belief that it was entirely possible to achieve his great dream. By the time Tiger was 25 years old, he was well on his way to becoming one of the greatest golfers in the history of the game. [3]

All of your future goals and dreams are not only a reflection of your subconscious thinking, they are mediated by your Reticular Activating System (RAS). The RAS is the part of your brain that serves as a filter between your conscious mind and your subconscious mind. The RAS, which is located in the core of your brain stem, takes instructions from your conscious mind, and passes them on to your subconscious mind.

Because of this biological function, whatever you are thinking about or focusing upon will seep down into your subconscious mind, only to reappear at a future time. Have you ever decided that you wanted to buy a certain car, and shortly thereafter, you see cars everywhere like the one you wanted? That is the RAS at work. [4]

From a very young age, Tiger Woods had begun the process of programming his mind to achieve his goals. There were several things that Tiger did to subconsciously create the future that he wanted...

1. He set a goal, and wrote it down.

2. He maintained a positive state of mind and attitude whenever he thought about his golfing dream.

3. He focused all of his attention on achieving that goal.

4. He set his intention to make it happen, and he believed that it was possible.

5. He also mentally rehearsed his goal over and over in his mind, as if it were a movie that had already happened.

KEYS TO MASTERING THE ART
OF BRINGFORTHISM

There are several ways to access the power of your subconscious mind for setting goals in the future. We call them the key elements of bringforthism. Some of these keys will be really obvious to you, and some of them won't be as obvious. The important thing to keep in mind is that if you try all of them, you can pretty much achieve any future goal or dream.

The first key element of bringforthism is to set a goal, and write it down. Writing your goal down will trigger your RAS, which in turn will send a signal to your cerebral cortex to stay focused on achieving the goal. The more clear and specific you can make your goal, the better the chances are that your subconscious mind will help you achieve it.[5]

In NLP there are four conditions for setting a well-formed goal:

1. Describe your goal in positive terms. Be certain to indicate what you do want, as opposed to what you don't want. You may want to ask, "Is my goal something that I want, or is it something that I don't want?" Rather than setting a goal to not be nervous during a job interview, you can set a goal for being calm and confident. Keeping the goal positive will help your RAS sort for feelings of calmness and confidence throughout your subconscious mind. If you set a goal to not be nervous, then the RAS will have to process being nervous first.

2. Ask yourself, "Is achieving the goal under my control, and can it be initiated by me?" Setting a goal for your boss to quit being a jerk is not a well-formed goal because you can't control what your boss does. The only thing you can control is your own behavior and attitude towards your boss. So instead, you could set a goal to be more assertive around your boss, or to ignore his behavior.

3. Define the sensory based evidence for achieving your goal. To do this, ask the following three questions:

- "How will you know when you have achieved your goal?"

- "What images, feelings, and sounds will you experience when you achieve your goal?"

- "If you were to run a movie of you achieving your goal, what would it look like?" Keep in mind that the more specific you can be, the better it is for your subconscious mind to help you achieve your goal.

4. Be ecological. Think about your goal, and define any possible downsides to achieving it. You may want to ask, "Who else might be affected when you 'bringforth' your goal into the future?"

For example, one of our clients named Steven set a goal to become a successful motivational speaker who traveled the country. Steven knew his goal was possible because he was already a talented speaker, however, his goal ended up not being so ecological. After setting his goal, Steven thought about its ecology and quickly realized that achieving his goal would have a negative impact on his two small children because of all the travel involved. He immediately decided not to do it because his children were more important to him than traveling around the country.

BRINGFORTHISM AND YOUR STATE OF MIND...

WHATEVER YOU THINK, YOU SHALL RECEIVE

The next key element of bringforthism has to do with your state of mind. This has to do with the emotional states that are connected to your goal. When you experience a positive state about achieving your goal, and stay focused on the outcome, you are sending a powerful message to your subconscious mind to bring-forth the desired goal. Have you ever noticed that when you are in a good mood and having a great day, people will smile at you more than they usually do? That is because you are sending your RAS a message to be happy, and so your subconscious mind will begin to pay attention to more positive experiences.

In his essay on *Compensation*, Ralph Waldo Emerson said, "Whatever you think, you shall receive."[6]

Your attitude, moods and feelings are energetic attractors for various life experiences. Each one of these elements serves as a driver for your state of mind. And your state of mind serves as a trigger for where you place your conscious attention, and what you choose to focus on. If you are in a bad mood, then you are more likely to place your attention on negative things, which will make it more difficult to achieve your goal.

Therefore, whatever you are feeling you will bringforth into your awareness because your outer reality is a reflection of your inner reality. If you stay focused on your goal, then your chances of achieving it will increase significantly, because you are sending a message to your RAS to filter its attention for the desired outcome.

One way to keep your attention on your goal while maintaining a positive state is to monitor your internal dialogue and thoughts. Because of your higher cognitive ability as a human, there is a tendency to be constantly talking to yourself about what is going on in the world outside of you, and how it impacts you. Sometimes, it is really easy to get into a negative space and not even realize it, because your ongoing internal thoughts and dialogue are outside of your conscious awareness. They are operating at a subconscious level, and are controlling the experiences that you bring forth, both positive and negative.

An easy way to become more conscious of your deeper sub-conscious thinking is to set your intent to be more consciously aware of your internal experience. You can do this by periodically checking in with yourself throughout the day to see how you are feeling emotionally. If you are having a good day, then chances are that you are maintaining a positive state of mind, and keeping your attention and focus on your goals for the day. If you find yourself wandering away from your goal and having a hard time staying focused on it, then you can ask your subconscious mind the following question,

"What is going on inside of me, and what is stopping me from achieving my goal?"

Interestingly, if you give your subconscious mind a moment to answer, it will tell you exactly what is going on in the form of a picture, a movie, or an internal commentary. You can then begin to communicate with this deeper subconscious part of yourself, and ask:

"What do I need to do to get more focused on my goal?"

Again, more often than not, your subconscious mind will give you the answer or solution. Sometimes, the solution is really simple, like perhaps you need to simply rest or take a break. Other times, it may be more complicated.

For example, we had a client named Barbara, whose goal was to start a new coaching and consulting business. Barbara's problem was that she was unable to take the necessary steps to bring her goal of starting a business into fruition. Every time she thought about doing the things she needed to do to start her business, she got overwhelmed and would place her attention on everything but her new business. Because of this, she got frustrated with the whole idea of starting a business and became depressed.

Finally, one day Barbara called us to see if we could help her regain her focus. She told us how overwhelmed and depressed she was by the whole idea of starting a new business. After listening to her for a few minutes, we asked her a really simple question:

"Take a minute to drop inside now and ask yourself, what is really stopping you from achieving this goal?" Barbara quietly sat there for a moment as she contemplated this question. After about a minute of thinking about it, tears started coming from her eyes, and she said,

"I finally realize why I have been so depressed about starting a business. Several years ago, I went into business with another woman and she horribly betrayed me. We ended up splitting up as business partners, and I had to take another job working for someone else. What I am realizing from this is that I still have a lot of anger toward her for what she did to me, and I need to forgive her and let go of that anger."

We then asked Barbara's subconscious mind another really simple question:

"What do you think the positive intention of your having anger is?" (In other words, "What is the good reason for you holding that anger?")

Again, Barbara got quiet and contemplative. As she began to think about her answer, we noticed that her face softened up and she didn't look so angry any more. Barbara then replied in a soft voice, "Well, I think the positive intention of my anger is that it was trying to protect me from something bad happening when I started my new business."

Barbara quickly realized that her subconscious anger was keeping her from maintaining a positive attitude and focus around her goal of starting a new business. We then asked Barbara's subconscious mind another question:

"What are some other ways that you can protect yourself, without having to be angry?"

She thought about this for a minute and got a big smile on her face saying, "Well, there are a lot of other ways that I can protect myself, such as paying better attention to the business records that I keep, and being more careful about who I do business with. I had a bad gut feeling about the woman who betrayed me, and I didn't listen to it. In the future, I will pay better attention to my internal thoughts and feelings."

Barbara then proceeded to outline a concrete business plan for starting a successful consulting business, which was the first time she was able to do so with clarity and peace of mind.

Barbara's inability to stay focused on her business goal was directly related to her deeper subconscious fear and anger around being betrayed. Once she gained conscious awareness of these feelings, she was then able to let go of the fear and anger and replace them with her own internal resources for protection. She did this by simply sorting for the positive intention of her subconscious anger, and then coming up with several solutions to insure that she would always be protected from any type of future betrayal.[7]

Thus, Barbara's subconscious mind was completely at peace with the idea of achieving her future goal of starting a successful coaching and consulting business. She was finally able to maintain a positive state of mind, while keeping her conscious attention and focus on her desired outcome.

THE POWER OF SETTING YOUR INTENT

Setting your intent is another key element for encouraging your subconscious mind to bring forth a desired goal. According to the Merriam-Webster Dictionary, the word "intent" is derived from the word "intend", which means, "to direct the mind and proceed on course towards a goal". The word "intent" originated from the Latin intendere, which means, "to stretch towards". When you set your intent, you are directing your RAS to stretch towards the goal, and to also enjoy the journey getting there.

To gain an experience with setting your intent, try saying the following three sentences to yourself:

1. "I hope to enjoy my dinner tonight." (Notice how you actually think about this—your internal pictures, voices, and feelings.)

2. "I want to enjoy dinner tonight." (Notice how you actually think about this—your internal pictures, voices, and feelings. What is different from the first sentence?")

3. "I intend to enjoy my dinner tonight." (Notice how you actually think about this—your internal pictures, voices, and feelings—what is different from the first two sentences?)

Pay attention to how each of these simple changes in your language creates a very different experience. For most people, the first sentence will produce some doubt. In other words, multiple images will appear in your mind representing different possibilities—one is that you may enjoy dinner and the other that you won't.

The second sentence should produce a different representation. When you say, "I want to enjoy dinner tonight," you will typically see what you want in the future, but you may not see yourself having it now. The future then may feel compelling because you see what you want. But there is still some room for doubt because it is more difficult to put yourself into the actual experience of achieving it.

The third image of intending to enjoy your dinner should put you into the act of fully enjoying your experience and being present to it. Intending for something to happen will generally associate you into the experience of achieving your goal and all the feelings, images and sounds that go with it.

When you set your intent, you are marrying your subconscious mind with your conscious will to make something happen. It is like you are sending your subconscious mind a message that you are expecting the event to happen, and there is absolutely no room for uncertainty.

Setting your intent is a way of preparing your subconscious mind for the kind of journey that you will have in achieving your goal. While setting your goal represents the end result you want to achieve. For example, Tiger Woods set a goal to become one of the greatest golfers in the world. He also set his intent to have as much fun as he could with playing golf. By staying focused on his goal and staying true to his intent, Tiger eventually achieved his desired goal while having a lot of fun along the way.

We originally learned about the idea of setting intent from a Peruvian shaman who we worked with years ago in the deserts of Southern Utah. We were with a group of NLP practitioners who were modeling the healing powers of the shaman. One of the men in the group, George, had the beginning symptoms of early multiple sclerosis, and asked the shaman if he would do a healing with him.

The shaman said, "Yes," and laid George down on the ground, and engaged him in a rather unusual healing ceremony. He first got a rattle out, and shook the rattle over the George's head, and chanted and sang for a long time. He then picked up the George's arm and gently spoke to it. He kept doing these kinds of activities for almost an hour.

Finally, the shaman looked at George and told him to stand up. He reached out his hand to help. When the shaman was finished, George stood up and proclaimed with excitement, "I feel a lot better!"

We were all pretty amazed by this, and asked the shaman, "When did the healing actually take place?"

The shaman looked really confused by our question and replied, "The healing took place took place when I set my intent. The rest was ceremony."

What the shaman meant by this comment is that when he was clear on his intent, it made it easier to achieve his goal of healing the man. Hence, the shaman recognized that if he and George entered into the same system, any change he made would be reflected in the bigger system including George's health.

In Systems Thinking, there is a presupposition that if one part of the system changes, then the rest of the system has to change. Anthropologist and systems thinker, Gregory Bateson, metaphorically addresses the power of intent from a systemic perspective in his book, *Steps to an Ecology of Mind*.

> "When the phenomenon of the universe is seen as linked together by cause and effect and energy transfer, the resulting picture is of a complexly branching and interconnecting chain of events. In certain regions of this universe (notably organisms in environments, ecosystems, societies, and computers), these chains of relating events form circuits which are closed in the sense that causal interconnection can be traced around the circuit and back through to whatever position we chose as the starting point of the description. In such a circuit, events at any position within the circuit may be expected to have an effect on all of the positions at later times."[8]

Setting your intent is a powerful way of directing your conscious energy and attention towards your future goal, which in turn helps your subconscious mind to stay focused on the desired outcome. Your subconscious mind and conscious mind are a system that co-exists within a larger system that we call reality. How we think, act, and behave has a direct influence on the greater system of our external reality. When we set our intent, we are influencing both our inner reality and our outer reality in a way that sets a chain of events into motion. We are bringing forth a new chain of events that are directly related to our deeper subconscious thinking, as well as our overall intent for the desired outcome and journey that unfolds.

Hence, the shaman was clear on the fact that the actual "healing ceremony" offered George's subconscious mind something to wrap this process around. The healing ritual or ceremony was a way to comfort George's subconscious mind, but the action took place systemically. If you change any part of a system, the rest of the system cannot not respond.

Not only does intent-setting work well with goals, it is also extremely useful to do throughout the day. For example, you might set your intent to find a parking space quickly and easily when trying to park your car in a crowded area. Or perhaps you have a big meeting with your boss and you want the meeting to run smoothly and effortlessly. You could then set your intent to be calm and to speak clearly throughout the meeting. Here is a real easy process for setting your intent around certain goals or situations:

1. Think of the goal or situation that you would like to set your intent for.

2. Set intent for yourself in terms of the experience that you want to have in that situation, or in achieving your goal.

3. If there are other people involved, then set your intent for the kind of interaction that you would like to have with them. Perhaps you would like to have fun, learn something new, be productive, feel peaceful, be happy or loving, feel respected, be calm and helpful, or feel connected with others.

4. Create a mental movie of what you will be like in that future situation. Notice what you are experiencing in the situation once you have set your intent. What are you hearing? What are you saying to yourself? What are you seeing and what are you feeling? [9]

REFERENCES

1. The word "bringforthism", coined by Tim and Kris Hallbom, originated from the years of research they had done in the fields of Systemic Thinking, NLP, and autopoiesis. They first came across the idea of bringforthism when reading an essay on autopoiesis. The term autopoiesis means, "self creating," and was originally introduced by Chilean biologists Francisco Varela and Humberto Maturana in the early 1970s. The Greek meaning of the prefix *auto* is "self" and refers to the autonomy of self-organizing systems such as the human mind. The Greek *poeire* means production or creation, such as poetry and refers to the ongoing creative process that exists within all living systems. Autopoiesis offers us a deeper understanding of the deeper structure of our human experience on this earth, which includes bridging the gap between the subconscious mind and the conscious mind. Autopoiesis also explores the internal occurrences that happen within a system and the parts that make up the system; the relationships between those parts; the boundaries that surround and contain the parts; how information emerges from the system via cognition; and how external information triggers the structure of the overall system.

2. In the field of NLP, a metaphor that we sometimes use for the subconscious and conscious minds is that of a flashlight in the attic. The attic is filled with interesting things that you can shine your flashlight on. Whatever the flashlight shines on is where your conscious awareness rests. Nevertheless, there are a lot of other things in that dark subconscious room, and you will be only conscious of what you see in the ray of the flashlight. The subconscious includes all these additional things that exist, yet are in the dark at the moment.

3. *The Tiger Woods Story* (1998) (TV)

4. *Write it down, Make it Happen* by Henriette Anne Klauser (Simon & Schuster, Inc., 2000).

5. The Well-Formedness Conditions originated in the field of NLP.

6. *Compensation, The Complete Works of Ralph Waldo Emerson - Volume II - Essays I* (1841)

7. "Positive intention" is a term often used in the field of NLP. It originated from the NLP presupposition that "Behind every behavior is a positive intention."

8. *Steps to an Ecology of Mind* by Gregory Bateson (Ballantine Books, a division of Random House, Inc., 1972)

9. The intent-setting process originated in the Wealthy-Mind™ program developed by Tim and Kris Hallbom in 2000.

10. .*The Tree of Knowledge: The Biological Roots of Human Understanding* by H.R. Maturana, and F. Varela. (Shambhala Publications, Inc., 1987).

About the Authors

TIM HALLBOM

Tim Hallbom is a world-renowned behavioral scientist. He knows just how to get inside people's minds and figure out how they do what they do. He has mastered the process of deconstructing human behavior and what people are doing inside their minds to achieve exceptional results. His easy manner and ability to connect with people has earned him a reputation as a true master among his peers. He is dedicated to helping everyday people and organizations achieve significantly more in their lives. Let him help you and your organization have a breakthrough experience at your next event.

Tim is a pioneer in Neuro-Linguistic Programming (NLP), which is a field dedicated to understanding human patterning. Throughout his extensive career, Tim has worked with individuals and organizations, authored several articles and books, founded training centers and professional organizations, keynoted international conferences, and lectured all over the world. He is a gifted speaker and trainer, and a genius in the area of peak performance and making personal change.

Tim is the Co-Founder and Behavioral Scientist of the Everyday Genius Institute, a company that deconstructs great minds and presents their strategies so that everyday people can achieve extraordinary results. He also trains at the NLP & Coaching Institute of California, a world-renowned organization dedicated to teaching people strategies for making personal change.

NICK LEFORCE

Nick LeForce has over 25 years experience of training in coaching and NLP programs and teaching others how to be highly effective in every area of their life. His genuine expertise plus engaging training style have made him highly sought after by business organizations and NLP institutes throughout the United States, Mexico and Asia. He is the author of several articles and books, including, *Co-Creation* (2009) and *I Owe, You Owe Me* (2006). He has also maintained a busy coaching practice for the last decade.

Nick holds a masters degree in rehabilitation administration from the University of San Francisco McLaren School of Business and undergraduate degrees in psychology and social welfare. Nick provides executive coaching services and management consultation to businesses, as well as personal development services to individuals. He helps individuals and businesses to identify governing values, and use those values to create compelling goals, make effective decisions, manage time, overcome barriers to success, communicate persuasively, and achieve desired outcomes.

Index

Resource List

BOOKS

Innovations in NLP, Hall, Michael; Charvet, Shelle Rose; Hallbom, Tim; Hallbom, Kris; Hollander, Jaap; McDermott, Ian; et. al., Crown House Publishing, 2011.

NLP: The New Technology of Achievement, Faulkner, Charles; Hallbom, Tim; Smith, Suzi; et. al., Harper, 1994.

Co-Creation: How to Collaborate for Results, LeForce, Nick, Messenger Mini-Book, 2009.

Beliefs: Pathways to Health and Well–Being, Dilts, Robert; Hallbom, Tim; and Smith, Suzi, Crown House Publishing, 2012.

The Life Coaching Handbook, Curley, Martin, Crown House Publishing, 2001.

Magic of NLP Demystified, Lewis, Byron and Pucelik, Frank, 2nd ed. Crown House Publishing, 2012.

Coach to Awakener, Dilts, Robert, Meta Publishers, 2007.

Your Inner Coach, McDermott, Ian and Jago, Wendy, Platkus Books, 2003.

Heaven In Our Hearts, Selected Poems by Nick LeForce, Inner Works, 2012.

I Owe You, You Owe Me: Breaking Free of Emotional Debt and Creating Abundant Relationships, LeForce, Nick, iUniverse, 2006.

DVD PROGRAMS

Journey Into the Structure of Beliefs and How You Create Your Reality, Hallbom, Tim; Dilts, Robert; and Hallbom, Kris, 2010 — Explores the origins of beliefs and how they impact us.

The WealthyMind, 4 DVD Set, Hallbom, Tim and Hallbom, Kris, 2008 — A complete two-day workshop on belief change and keys for successful living.

Dynamic Spin Release, 2 DVD Set, Hallbom, Tim and Hallbom, Kris, 2009 — Learn simple yet powerful techniques for creating useful change.

Think Like a Genius Core Strategies, Hallbom, Tim, Everyday Genius Institute, 2010 — Seven Techniques to unlock your inner genius.

Visit Tim Hallbom on the web: http://www.nlpca.com, http://www.thewealthymind.com, and http://www.dynamicspinrelease.com

Visit Nick LeForce on the web: http://www.transformationalpoet.com

Made in the USA
Lexington, KY
16 April 2014